Are We Preaching "Another" Gospel?

A 31-day Journey toward Rediscovering the Gospel of the Grace of God

Grace & Peace to You! cdh

By
C. D. Hildebrand

XULON PRESS

Are We Preaching "Another" Gospel?
A 31-day Journey toward Rediscovering the Gospel
of the Grace of God
by C. D. Hildebrand

Printed in the United States of America

ISBN 9781628713619

The author has chosen not to use gender-specific pronouns unless specifically indicated, as she finds writing and reading "he/she" and "him/her" to be tedious. If, as a woman, you find this offensive, as a woman, I sincerely apologize.

www.xulonpress.com

This book is dedicated
to my dearly beloved husband, David,
who is my closest companion
in life and ministry,
to my children and grandchildren
who fill my heart with daily joy and love,
and to all of those
who are determined
to preach the gospel,
the whole gospel,
and NOTHING but the gospel.

Table of Contents

Are We Preaching "Another" Gospel?

A 31-day Journey toward Rediscovering the Gospel of the Grace of God

What We Believe and Teach

For more information about our ministry, please visit our website.[1]

- *There is one God, eternally preexistent as God the Father, God the Son, and God the Holy Spirit; that is to say, we believe in the Trinity of God. This God is love and deeply loves mankind whom He has created. He demonstrates His love for all by giving His Son to die for us that whoever believes in Him will not perish but have everlasting life (Romans 5:8; John 3:16).*
- *Each original word of Scripture in both the Old and New Testaments was given by inspiration of God, is relevant to believers today, and must be interpreted in context, its original significance, and in light of the New Covenant (2 Peter 1:19-21; 2 Timothy 3:16-17; 2 Peter 3:15-16).*
- *Jesus was born of a virgin, lived a sinless life, was crucified, died, and bodily rose from the dead in order to eternally redeem those who would believe in Him and confess Him as the Lord. He lived on earth fully man and fully God, and He is the only mediator between man and God. The work of the cross of Christ was God's complete work upon which no improvement can be made by man (Romans 10:9-10; Hebrews 9:12; 1*

---

[1] http://www.graceandfaithministries.org

Timothy 2:5; John 19:30; Colossians 2:9-10; Hebrews 10:14; Galatians 3:3).

•*The commandments of the New Covenant are that we believe in the name of God's Son, Jesus Christ, and love one another. Believing in His Son and loving one another, are our highest expressions of love for God (1 John 3:23; Matthew 25:40; John 14:21; John 21:15).*

•*We are saved by grace alone through faith in Christ alone, initially (at salvation), continually (in this life), and eventually (at His return). While believers are created for good works, they are not saved by them (Ephesians 2:8-10; Titus 3:4-6).*

•*Our behavior is a fruit of our imputed right-standing with God. Since we are freed from sin and made holy, blame-less, and righteous by faith, we are motivated to live a holy life. When we fall short, the blood of Jesus Christ cleanses us from all sin (Romans 5:17; Romans 6:1-14; Galatians 5:22; Colossians 1:21-23; Romans 6:22; 1 John 2:1; 1 John 1:7).*

•*At the moment of salvation Jesus Christ lives inside of believers by faith and they are seated in heavenly places with Christ Jesus. All believers dwell continually in God's presence and His presence dwells continually in them because of the blood of Christ and they are full sons of God by faith in Jesus Christ. (Colossians 1:27; Ephesians 2:6; Hebrews 4:14-16; Galatians 3:26).*

•*All of the gifts and ministry gifts in operation in the Early Church are available to believers today and are to be manifested "decently and in order" by grace through faith alone (Acts 2:38-39; Galatians 3:2-5; Romans 11:29).*

•*We believe in the final resurrection of both the saved and the lost; the former to eternal life and latter to eternal judgment; (Revelation 20:11-15; John 3:17-18)*

•*We believe in the imminent return of Jesus Christ; the Rapture of the Church (1 Thessalonians 4:13-18; 1 Corinthians 15:50-55).*

Foreword

Here is what those who have read <u>Are We Preaching "Another" Gospel?</u> have to say.

The moment I met Cathy Hildebrand and her husband, David, I knew that we shared a kindred heart for the gospel of God's unfathomable grace. Now I am delighted to be able to recommend this incredible book to my friends and every believer who has ever felt like the Jesus they originally fell in love with was somehow hijacked by man-made philosophies and burdensome religious superstition. <u>Are We Preaching "Another" Gospel?</u> is a clear and compassionate call for believers everywhere—including pastors and leaders—to honestly evaluate whether we are truly believing and preaching the gospel of Jesus and the apostles. We can certainly agree to disagree about many things in the big tent of Christianity, but if we get the gospel wrong, the consequences are too great to ignore. Don't just read this book. Meditate upon its content. Study it with your Bible in hand. See if my friend Cathy isn't on to something huge here. I think you'll agree that she is...and it matters...a lot!

Jeremy White
Pastor and Author of <u>The Gospel Uncut: Learning to</u>
<u>Rest in the Grace of God</u>

The question, "Are we preaching 'another' gospel?" to me as a layperson who studies to show herself approved, but who sits in the sanctuary rather than preaches from the podium, translated to, "Am I *believing* 'another' gospel?" My cousin, Cathy's book compelled me to search deeper in both my King James Study Bible and into my own heart and mind. Ever vigilant to avoid entertaining false doctrines, I read Are We Preaching "Another" Gospel? ready to argue every assertion. The book challenged me to question if my belief and practice of Grace by Faith aligns with Scripture and to seek God to open my eyes and my spirit, to provide me discernment in His word, the Gospel, and in my faith and His grace. While often I disagreed and argued and once even thought I would not read another word, I still was spiritually urged to continue to read and search the Scriptures for the truth of Grace by Faith. Throughout my reading I was amazed at how much more time I spent in my Bible, seeking either confirmation or refutation of what I was reading. In the end, I realized how much I enjoyed the spiritual exercise and how much stronger I had become in His Word, in Grace by Faith, the Gospel of Christ, and most of all, my gratefulness for the Cross and the Blood of the Lamb. Thank you, Jesus for the manger, the cross, and the Gospel. I would run this marathon again.

Nancy Morin
Sincere Follower of Christ

Cathy and I have been close friends since the third grade. I know in my heart that the Lord put her in my life and I feel blessed and proud to say our friendship is still wonderful 52 years later. More importantly to me, Cathy has guided me through the years in my pursuit to learning the true meaning of Scripture. Growing up in a Catholic family, I was taught to fear God, continually ask for forgiveness of sins, and that salvation is earned. Even though I felt God's love, I questioned a lot of the teachings of the Catholic

Church, and always felt as if "something" was missing. The "something" came in the way of Cathy sharing grace through faith with me. I studied Scripture in the New Testament carefully, and prayed for complete understanding of the gospel of Jesus and the apostles. Over time I came to realize the true meaning of Christianity and carry a joy in my heart I cannot describe. How had I been incorporating man-made laws that I could never accomplish on my own? How could this have happened, and how many Christians are out there experiencing the same thing? Living in a world where we are constantly told to do our best in order to reap our reward cannot apply to God. We can never earn our own salvation and Cathy brilliantly argues this point in her book <u>Are We Preaching "Another" Gospel?</u> through Scripture.

This book is a must read for all searching to understand what Jesus accomplished for us when He died on the cross, and the simple, but perfect plan He calls His believers to follow. I am grateful for her careful study of Scripture and how she challenges all of us, including pastors, and spiritual leaders, to make sure we are preaching the true gospel. Thank you, Cathy, for writing this book.

Your loving friend and sister in Christ,
Linda Atme

Out of the midst of traditional, "stench of death" religion arises a sweet fragrance of liberty declaring the beautiful simplicity of Christ in us, the hope of glory! Skillfully written by Cathy Hildebrand, <u>Are We Preaching "Another" Gospel?</u> confirms the heart-cry of believers around the world! May this instrument be refreshing breath, clear vision, and freedom to the body of Christ!

Carolyn Graham
Co-Pastor of Narrow Way Ministries, Roswell,
New Mexico

Uncle Dave and Aunt Cathy (the author) led me to Christ 33 years ago. I am forever grateful. When my aunt asked me to read this book I was both honored and a little skeptical—honored because she is my aunt and skeptical because she comes from an Assemblies of God perspective and my seminary training is Baptist. Regardless, there is much we agree on when it comes to the importance of grace through Jesus Christ's death and resurrection as the only and completely sufficient way to salvation and freedom from the tyranny of legalism. Her analysis and arguments are well-researched and her passion undeniable. Are We Preaching "Another" Gospel? is worth the time to consider the importance of grace and the danger of teaching works as the way to please God or earn His favor.

Rick Pierce
M.Div., Western Seminary

Are We Preaching "Another" Gospel? is an excellent resource for anyone interested in the fullness and goodness of God's grace. Christian laymen, pastors, elders and small-group leaders alike will benefit greatly from the insights Cathy shares.

This book will help you dig out from much of the legalism and traditions under which we find ourselves buried in our walk with God. "Preaching the gospel of grace to the saved" may seem unnecessary to many at first glance; it did to my wife and me. But being reminded of "the grace of the Lord Jesus Christ, and the love of God, and the fellowship of the Holy Spirit" has helped us return to our first love. Once again we have the joy and peace we knew when we first came to Jesus. Living the abundant life Jesus promised is possible, and our eternal life starts now not sometime in the hereafter. Jesus and the New Covenant make all of this and more a reality in our daily lives.

David Graybiel
Ministry Team Member for Studies in Grace and Faith

*Research Consultant, Christian Answers & Information,
a former cults and apologetics ministry
Former faculty member, Calvary Chapel Bible College,
Chico extension campus*

As a Christian and a minister, I have been following the "Grace" teachings for 25 years. The Grace/Gospel/New Covenant message radically changed my life and relationship with God. <u>Are We Preaching "Another" Gospel?</u> is the clearest and most understandable presentation of the many facets of the gospel that Jesus died to give us that I have read so far. This book is a "must read" and a "must study" book for any Christian minister or teacher who has the privilege to teach THE gospel of Jesus. This book is not just for ministers though, as it is written clearly enough for anyone who wants to see the beauty and depths of Jesus and His completed mission. Every minister should have their staff and congregations read this book. Lives will be changed from knowing and understanding the gospel which is the power of God.

"Are We Preaching "Another" Gospel?" was born out of Cathy's passion for the truth that sets people free and to expose the errors that bind us. She is one of the most diligent and honest students of the Bible that I have known or observed in my 39 years of being a Christian and a minister. For 38 of those years I have had the blessing and privilege of knowing her as my best friend and partner in life and ministry. Thank you, Cathy, for writing this great work, and for being the true love of my life.

*David Hildebrand
Beloved Husband
Pastor, Teacher
Co-Founder of Studies in Grace and Faith*

Acknowledgements

*M*y mother, being a pastor's child in the 1920-40s, was raised in a super legalistic environment which made her determined to raise me with an abundance of grace. I knew God's grace and hers every day of my life. She loved me when I didn't deserve it and spoke of His love for me by every word and deed of hers. Her love allowed me to love my children the same way even when I was being taught contrarily about God's love for me. I have never known human love so beautiful and complete as my mother's, Enid Bennett Whitt (1922-1984).

I want to profoundly thank Bob George for saving my husband's life in 1989 through his radio broadcast and his book, <u>Classic Christianity</u>. You own a very special place in our hearts. Thank-you for giving us permission to believe that the gospel is truly as good as it is.

To those who braved to read and/or edit my manuscript, thank-you so much. Your input was encouraging and treasured: Linda Atme, Nancy Morin, Rick Pierce, Jeremy White, Carolyn Graham, and David Graybiel.

For our beloved friends who are working with us to share this message, we thank you for your love, support, and encouragement. You know who you are!

Finally, I want to express that I am so blessed and so thankful for my husband of 38 years. We have been working closely together throughout our marriage in ministry to family and in ministry to the body of Christ. Although David does most of the speaking and I do most of the writing, we both study independently and together when assembling our teachings. We appreciate and value each other's callings and gifts and treasure how God combines them together to create something beautiful.

The ideas I share here reflect both of our beliefs; however, when I was finally ready to write this book, David graciously stepped aside and let me spread my wings and fly "solo". He has been my biggest supporter during this time of writing, encouraging me and calming my fears. I love you, David, and thank God for bringing us together. You will always be my dearest friend.

So, in view of all of those who have contributed to this book and who work with us in sharing the good news with God's beloved people, I'd like to say:

Ecclesiastes 4:9-12

Two are better than one,

Because they have a good reward for their labor.

[10] For if they fall, one will lift up his companion.

But woe to him who is alone when he falls,

For he has no one to help him up.

[11] Again, if two lie down together, they will keep warm;

But how can one be warm alone?

[12] Though one may be overpowered by another,

Two can withstand him.

And a threefold cord is not quickly broken.

Prologue

*I*f you are looking for a book that is hostile toward pastors or one which seeks to defame the organized church, this book is not for you. I feel I need to say this up front for two reasons. One, I want pastors to read this book. When I wrote it, you were on my heart and mind. I want you to know that as former pastors, my husband and I deeply respect you and what you are called to do. While I disagree with what is commonly being taught in churches today, you will not find within these pages anything but respect concerning your calling and labor of love.

The second reason I want to make the above perfectly clear is I don't want this book to fan the flames of anger commonly felt by some who wake to realize that their beloved teachers pointed them in a wrong direction; a path that likely caused pain and even devastation. If this describes you, please consider this. When you were ill-taught, you had a Bible. You had a brain. You chose to believe what ended up binding you. Ultimately, we are each responsible to "prove all things and hold fast to that which is good". I urge you to work toward forgiveness so that you may share the message of the gospel of grace—with grace.

Being a user of social media, I am continually reminded that written communication apart from relationship falls miserably short at times. In discussing, even disagreeing with someone who knows and loves you well, the writer has an advantage which contributes greatly to the possibility of being "heard" even if the topic is controversial as I understand this topic to be.

An example of this was evidenced with my most critical proof reader—in the good sense, who strongly disagreed with me as she began to read, painstakingly commenting to me throughout my manuscript her questions, comments, and concerns; but knowing me and loving me as she does, she pressed forward and was able to understand more fully the question I am asking.

Ideally, I could sit down with each person reading this and talk with you as you read as I did with my friend above, answering questions as they arise, and discussing difficult concepts. However, written communication doesn't allow for such. Thanks for your patience. When you finish the book, please join the discussion on Facebook at https://www.facebook.com/cdhildebrandgrace.

Another major concern of mine while writing and editing this book was the same one our nephew, Rick, also a minister, pointed out to me—specifically that *he* knew what I was saying because we discussed these things over the years, but he wondered if someone who had never considered this topic would follow my points unless I clarified them more fully. This is why every effort has been made to present this topic as if the reader has never heard it before (or who hasn't heard it in many years) but hopefully without insulting the intelligence of those who likely possess degrees far higher and knowledge more extensive than I ever will. It might help to know that in the early chapters of the book ideas are introduced that are expounded upon later.

I am deeply dependent on the fact that all believers have the Holy Spirit dwelling within them and that He is speaking to each of our hearts. If what I am saying is true, He will be in the reader's heart affirming that truth. If I have erred, He will point that out, too. Though, of course, I *believe* what I have written *is* true, I do not pretend to "know it all".

So, please allow me to introduce myself. My name is Cathy Hildebrand. I am a daughter of God, wife of David, aside and explained the way of the Lord to him more accurately.

Thank-you for considering this topic and for having a heart that is willing to learn.

Sincerely in Him,

C. D. Hildebrand

Introduction

Several years ago during the Sunday morning worship time, I found myself once again with my face in my hands praying that the song we were singing would get over sooner than later. It was one of those repetitive melodies that we'd sung so many times I was beginning to fall into a mental stupor. Admittedly, this wasn't the best attitude for someone of my age and maturity, but perhaps you can imagine, in light of what was about to occur, the humor of my anguish.

It was in that frame of mind when suddenly, one of those crystal clear moments broke through; when I heard God speak sweetly to my heart. It actually surprised me since my prayer had nothing to do with seeking the will of God for my life, but was something more along the lines of, "Lord, please make them STOP!"

He asked, "Are you willing—"

Now, there was no pause in the upcoming question, but I remember a split-second moment of being aware He was not only *speaking* to me, but was going to call me to do something, and a certain surprised anticipation rose up within me. He had my attention! God was getting through to me even through all the noise and frustration in my mind. As I listened carefully, my heart immediately began answering when He said, "Are you willing to preach the gospel to the *saved*?"

Knowing instantly what He meant, I replied, "Yes, Lord. I am willing." Sitting there somewhat stunned and entirely delighted and amazed, I could hardly wait to tell my husband, David, who then embraced this calling as one for the both of us. Since that moment, this is what we have dedicated ourselves to do; to sharing the gospel with God's beloved children.

Why do the *saved* need to hear the gospel?

"Let him who has ears to hear, hear."

But by the grace of God
I am what I am,
and His grace toward me
was not in vain;
but I labored
more abundantly than they all,
yet not I,
but the grace of God which was with me.

1 Corinthians 15:10

But none of these things move me;
nor do I count my life dear to myself,
so that I may finish my race
with joy,
and the ministry
which I received
from the Lord Jesus,
to testify to the
gospel of the
grace of God.

Acts 20:24

I marvel that you are turning away so soon
from Him who called you
*in the **grace of Christ**,*
*to a **different gospel**,*
⁷ which is not another;
but there are some who trouble you
*and want to **pervert the gospel** of Christ.*
⁸ But even if we, or an angel from heaven,
*preach **any other gospel** to you*
than what we have preached to you,
*let him be **accursed**.*
⁹ As we have said before, so now I say again,
*if anyone preaches **any other gospel** to you*
than what you have received,
*let him be **accursed**.*

Galatians 1:6-9

Day 1

ARE WE PREACHING "ANOTHER" GOSPEL?

---

*P*ersonally, I find no delight in the idea of being *accursed*. I'm guessing you agree.

Until 1987, Galatians 1:6-9 meant something completely different to my husband and me than it does today. When we read these verses we exclusively attributed them to the cults. Of course cults would be accursed, we reasoned, because they were preaching a different Jesus than the one presented in Scripture. We studied the side-by-side comparisons and knew the major theological differences. In our thinking, anyone who messed with God's gospel *should* be accursed.

We never considered for one minute that *we* would fall into the category of preaching "another" gospel.

The question I am posing in this book to my fellow ministers and to the church as a whole is very important to consider. **Are we, the church, preaching "another" gospel?** For since teaching "another" gospel comes with being accursed and leads God's people astray, it makes perfect sense to extensively consider the question.

I will be honest about my perspective—that much of what is being taught in "mainstream" Christian churches today is "another" gospel. Coming to this conclusion about 25 years ago was a *very painful* process because we discovered that we were among those preaching "another". Since then we have re-examined just about everything we thought we knew, and I'd like to share with you what we believe the Lord taught us.

There could not have been more sincere hearts than ours those fourteen years before we woke up to find that our belief system was "another". We were born again believers and our love for God and our commitment to serving Him was unwavering. We entered ministry at a young age and not only taught with passion and conviction what we believed, but endeavored to be "real" and loving with those to whom we ministered. However, it is possible to be sincere and possess good motives, even to be loving and authentic and still be mistaken.

Even before this realization that we had jumped the tracks theologically, nine years earlier in 1978; the Holy Spirit tried to get through to me while I was studying the book of Galatians. While reading it one day I sensed that there was something I was missing about what Paul was trying to communicate. I remember saying to my husband, "It doesn't seem right that when I pray and read my Bible each day, I feel justified before God, and when I don't, I don't." Why did reading Galatians provoke in me these thoughts? Surely there was nothing wrong with reading my Bible and praying for an hour each day—was there?

I remember calling the wife of our former associate pastor who preached very fervently about the importance of a consistent prayer life and time spent in the Bible (along with an ever-increasing list of other "disciplines"). I asked her if she was actually able to do all the things he taught.

What she said truly surprised me. "Well, no, not really, but I'm working on it."

While I appreciated her sweet and honest response, it seemed odd to me—that not even the pastor's wife, someone I held in such high regard, could keep up with all the expectations we were taught. Perhaps it should have given me some comfort knowing I wasn't the only one struggling, yet the idea still persisted that certain behaviors were *expected* of believers which somehow contributed to our "rightness" before God. At that same time in my life, another quandary confronted me. Why was it that after only four years of serving the Lord as an adult, now already in ministry, I felt *miserable* as a believer—so wretched, in fact, that just the idea of witnessing to my father saddened me thinking of how awful and unhappy being a Christian would eventually make his life? How could I tell someone who seemed to be enjoying each day of his existence golfing, fishing, and drinking with his buddies, that coming to Jesus would be so wonderful, when I knew he'd eventually feel as horrible as I did? Obviously, something was wrong with feeling that way, and yet it didn't seem right to *lie* to him. These thoughts caused me considerable confusion. Did I really think my father would be better off spending eternity in hell instead of becoming a believer in Jesus Christ? How absurd and illogical! Red flags were waving everywhere deep in my soul, but I couldn't figure it out.

It wasn't that my love for the Lord had grown cold. I still loved Jesus as deeply as ever. In fact, He miraculously healed our newborn daughter of a life-threatening condition just months before. I loved Him profoundly and was so thankful, but was discovering that even though I loved Jesus and greatly enjoyed being in Christian ministry; I didn't particularly like being a *Christian*. The whole situation had me completely baffled.

Afraid to ask these questions of our pastors for fear of being labeled "rebellious", and not wanting to be guilty of "touching God's anointed", I very privately mused over these concerns. Being a pillar in the church and someone the pastors could count upon was so important to David and me. What if they thought I was compromising? Others had been marginalized for going against what the leadership believed. Plus, what if my thoughts were just passing ones? What if post-partum depression was to blame? Perhaps I was simply experiencing burn-out. It wouldn't be worth the risk if these were the case. So out of fear of being misunderstood, the horror of experiencing rejection, the possibility that I might put my husband's full-time job as the college and youth pastor in jeopardy, and the chance that I was wrong, my questions remained unanswered.

It would be nine more years of living with this underlying dissatisfaction before I could begin to see what happened to that glorious "relationship" I knew the "hour I first believed".

During those long and dry years that followed, prayer, Bible study, and diligent service continued to be part of my spiritual life. All the while it seemed to me that God was getting farther away and that His love for me was only doctrinally understood. I had pretty much adapted to thinking that the "life" I was experiencing was all there was to being a Christian, and determined in my heart that the mature thing to do was to simply "walk by faith and not by sight". So, the questions and lack of joy in the Lord continued to be disregarded all those years while I focused on ministry to family and the church. I sincerely do not know how I could have endured that time if it were not for the joy of being a mom to the dearest children on earth. At least I knew *they* loved me and spending time with them brought me great joy.

During that time, I completed the educational requirements and passed the examination for ordination with our denomination. Surely the process of studying the Bible more in-depth and becoming an ordained minister would bring some contentment and a sense of purpose back into my Christian experience. Yet, on the night of my ordination ceremony, when the "mantle" was placed on my shoulders, I felt as numb spiritually as ever. This moment which I fully hoped would be as powerful of an experience for me as it had seemed to be for others, fell devastatingly flat. The anointing I heard about and anticipated descending upon me was painfully absent. The only thing imparted to me on that night was more disappointment.

None of this made sense to me; none at all. My love *for* God was so real to me. I was convinced of my calling to ministry. Each and every thought and deed was for Him and to Him, but His love for *me* felt obscured. From the outside, people saw a sincere and loving woman who lived what she taught; a good wife and mother who worked closely with her husband in ministry, a friend who was there in time of need, and a respected member of her community. I was consistent in spiritual disciplines and was careful to put others ahead of myself. As far as I knew, I wasn't sinning or even wanting to sin. So, why was there this sense that something was *terribly wrong*, that something was *devastatingly missing*?

God was not to blame, of course. That thought never entered my mind. If there was a problem, it would be with me not Him. My heart's cry was, "God, as far as I know I'm doing everything You want me to do, so why do You feel so far away and why does it seem You don't love me anymore? Is there something *more* You want from me? Have You put me on the shelf for a season? Have I committed some sin I have not confessed? Please help me to see what's wrong. Whatever You want from me, Lord, I am willing. I believe You will show me."

At that moment it was impossible for me to see the truth—that I'd been taught, embraced, and was beginning to teach "another" gospel. It was the reason I felt estranged from Christ and why I didn't have a sense of His love for me. I had fallen from grace in the true sense of the word.

Galatians 5:4
*You have become **estranged from Christ**, you who attempt to be **justified by law**; you have **fallen from grace**.*

Consider this for a minute: what if *you,* like we, were taught and believed and were now preaching "another" gospel and didn't know it? Wouldn't that be important to discover? Wouldn't you want someone to lovingly pull you aside and share with you the truth that would set you free?

That is why I'm writing this—to speak the truth in love to God's dearly beloved church. Even though sometimes "the truth hurts", I believe God's desire is to bring comfort and freedom. As ministers of the gospel, my husband and I pour our hearts and souls into everything we do, and I am assuming you are doing the same. I am not challenging for one minute your motivation, your dedication, or your labor of love. What I hope to accomplish is to help you discover whether *or not* you are believing and preaching "another" gospel by sharing with you what we learned—about how we took a wrong turn in our belief system and how learning the truth about the true gospel, set us free. It not only set us free, but is liberating those whom we now teach.

Ephesians 4:11-16

*And He Himself gave some to be apostles, some prophets, some evangelists, and some pastors and teachers, ¹² for the equipping of the saints for the work of ministry, for the edifying of the body of Christ, ¹³ **till we all come to the unity of the faith and of the knowledge of the Son of God**, to a perfect man, to the measure of the stature of the fullness of Christ; ¹⁴ that we should **no longer be children**, tossed to and fro and carried about with every wind of **doctrine**, by the trickery of men, in the cunning craftiness of deceitful plotting, ¹⁵ but, **speaking the truth in love**, may grow up in all things into Him who is the head—Christ— ¹⁶ from whom the whole body, joined and knit together by what every joint supplies, according to the effective working by which every part does its share, causes growth of the body for the edifying of itself in love.*

Day 2

ANSWERED PRAYER

*I*t is difficult to perceive what is causing one's problems
and impossible to recover from them, if one believes that
what she's doing to rid herself of her problems are actually
the source of them. In my case, God lovingly removed these
"good" things from my life so that I could return to the "one"
thing that was needful.

It was not too long after I asked God to show me why He
seemed far and why I couldn't feel His love that our lives took
an unexpected turn. I'm convinced now that these events
were God's answer to my heart's cry. Our ministry as home
missionaries ended, and even though we tried, we could not
find a new full-time paid ministry. This was a curious reality
for us as we had only ever seen ourselves continuing in ministry the rest of our lives. Needing to support three growing
children, we made the difficult decision to get secular jobs
and move to Southern California where we'd heard for years
of all the great churches in that area. Thankfully, I had all the
educational requirements I needed to be employed as an
emergency credentialed teacher in downtown Los Angeles,
and my husband began to be trained as a financial planner.

My new life in L.A. was extremely demanding. I had to
rise between 5:00 and 6:00 a.m. to get ready for work so I
could hopefully beat the traffic and arrive in my classroom
by 7:00. In order to work with an emergency credential, it
was also required that I take classes toward a full credential
after work. Each afternoon I would come home, cook dinner,

help the kids, and put them to bed; working often until 1:00 a.m. doing my own homework and preparing for the next school day. It didn't take long for me to notice that I had no time to pray and no time to read the Bible and that this situation was not going to change any time soon.

Though we tried each week, we were unable to find a church for several months. At first, we thought for sure that a church in our denomination would find out that we were ordained ministers and put us to work at least as volunteers, but no pastor took any interest in us at all, not even to befriend us, some even seemed to treat us with suspicion. It was our first time in thirteen years that we were not actively involved in ministry—and we couldn't even find a church home.

Being a stay-at-home mom became impossible since my income became our mainstay. It seemed that each and every dollar we earned was needed for bills. It was the first time ever that we could not tithe, let alone give anything extra. Our marriage was stressed. *Everything* that ever defined me as a good Christian woman was gone and seemed completely unattainable!

All of those people with whom we'd worked for so many years, who we thought loved us and might care about how difficult our life had become, seemed to distance themselves from us. None of them called to ask how it was going or to see if we needed help. It felt as if they were sitting back watching, expecting that we would fall from the Lord now that we'd left their protective covering. This was particularly painful for my husband who had only ever desired to be an active minister, but who now couldn't even find fellowship. He felt that everyone, including God, was displeased and disappointed in him.

One morning, while feeling troubled about the fact that I was failing God in every way, I said a prayer while getting into my car to go to work. "Jesus, You understand that I don't have time to pray." Now, what was in the back of my mind was that God would grant me a temporary reprieve until I got my teaching credential and my life would settle down a bit, then I'd go back to my normal routine of spiritual disciplines. "So,

Lord, I'm asking you to allow me to pray while driving to work." You might consider this to be odd if you have never lived under this type of thinking, but my understanding of "prayer" was that daily devotions were to be at a time and place set apart while doing *nothing* else. In my thinking, praying in my car while precariously maneuvering through downtown L.A. traffic clearly would not count as a "quiet time".

However, as I put my car in drive, I unknowingly ventured to where I hadn't been in many years. God had me exactly where He wanted me. **Though I could not have put it into these words at the time, I once again came to God empty-handed with faith in His grace to hear me.** The second I opened my mouth to pray with this frame of mind, the presence of God seemed to flood my car and overwhelmed my heart with His love for me. I wept all the way to school in utter amazement and full of joy along with feeling particularly baffled thinking something along the lines of, "What just happened?" It was what I'd been missing, the sense of His presence and knowing He loved me, and I had no idea what was going on or why this was coming about because *I hadn't done anything* to merit this outpouring of His love upon me. I simply did not deserve it. While completely delighted by this moment, I worried that it might be a one-time event or that I was being led astray!

The next few weeks were like I'd been born again, again. I was clueless as to why I was experiencing His precious love and presence because I wasn't *doing* anything. This caused me to reevaluate my concept of prayer and to reconsider the questions about which I'd mused nine years earlier—the questions I left unanswered out of fear. The sense of His closeness never left me and He began to answer all of my prayers, even the tiny short ones that weren't supposed to "count".

I tried to share what I was experiencing with my husband, but he would only look at me with a blank expression. All I could say to him; and I said it with considerable fear and trepidation, was that I was beginning to question what we'd been taught about prayer. Since I didn't really understand it, I was not very good at explaining myself, and he listened without hearing me. I was experiencing a very personal awakening hoping with all my heart it would not disappear as suddenly as it came, but David seemed to be in a soundproof room. I was knocking on the window and shouting this good news, but he could not hear me. What I didn't understand was that David was living through the deepest anguish of his life.

About a year later, after having moved back to Northern California, my husband came to a point of total despair. It wasn't that he didn't love Jesus. He did, but he didn't want anything to do with the religion of Christianity. He admitted to me one day that he had fantasized about driving off of one of the bridges in our area. The reason for this was that he perceived that God was disappointed and disgusted with him, and he had no idea how to do more than he'd already done in order to please Him. His best was clearly *not* good enough. Now David was exactly where God needed him to be.

Right around this time, he began to tune in to a daily live radio broadcast by Bob George called "People to People". When at first he would listen, he knew Bob was saying something different from what he believed, but he couldn't figure it out. It was as if there was a thick wall between them, and he couldn't understand the words. For about two months he listened every day, and gradually, he began to "get" it. He prayed, "God! I wish that what Bob is saying were *true*! I wish that being a Christian could be as good as he says. I wish You were as good as he is saying You are." As David continued to listen, what Bob was teaching came increasingly into focus for him until finally he just saw it. He ordered his recently published book, <u>Classic Christianity: Life is Too Short to Miss the Real Thing</u>, which continued to convince him that God *is* as good as He says He is, and he was able to recapture that love he'd known when he first put His faith in Jesus.

After this, David and I began a journey to figure out how we got off track as our determination grew to ***never ever*** go back the way we had gone—wherever that was. It was as if we'd been awakened from a very long dream, not even knowing we'd fallen asleep. We were completely surprised. How did this happen to us—we who had so deeply loved God, so earnestly sought Him, so greatly longed to please Him, and who had given our all to follow Him?

At first we thought it was just he and I who'd taken a wrong turn in our doctrine, but as time went by, we realized that we believed what we did because we received what we'd been taught. Thinking then that it was only our former church that was teaching error, we began to visit other churches in our denomination or churches with similar beliefs. To our great dismay, the same mixed messages were also being taught within other "full-gospel"[3] churches. Surmising that it was a tendency in Pentecostal churches to teach these things, we ventured out into non-Pentecostal churches. Amazingly, we kept hearing the same things there also. We weren't sure exactly what we wanted, but we did know what we no longer believed, and it was being preached *everywhere*!

We didn't know how to effectively communicate what was happening to us because in those days we could only express ourselves in these terms: what we no longer believed. We were beginning to realize again that being a Christian did not amount to a long list of things we needed to do, but a living and loving relationship with Jesus. As we began to share our experience with our close friends, they thought we had lost our minds or were "backsliding" and gradually withdrew from us.[4]

The next twenty years were spent raising our children, allowing God to untie multiple knots of error that held us bound, and rediscovering that the gospel really is "*glad* tidings of *good* things".

---

[3] If ever there was a misnomer, it would be "full-gospel".
[4] We are thrilled to report that those who misunderstood us have also had their own grace awakenings.

Day 3

THE TIME OF OUR VISITATION

*H*ave you been praying for revival? Many believers do. What images does the word "revival" bring to your mind? Do you see non-believers flocking to Christ for salvation and filling up the church to overflowing? Perhaps you superimpose revivals of the past into modern-day settings; sinners falling on their faces repenting of sin and whole cities being won to Jesus. We saw revival as an outpouring of the Holy Spirit in which supernatural manifestations of the presence of God would occur to the right and to the left; healings, signs and wonders, and believers overcome with God's power as our shadows passed by them.

We were told that we were "the" generation who would finally bring revival! It was inferred that the older generation of Christians was somehow less spiritual, but "we" were the elect of God. It was up to us to finally make revival happen. This talk puffed us up with a sort of prideful hope, but being the "chosen ones" we accepted the challenge placed before us. Bringing about revival was one of the main goals in our Christian walk. Our generation fasted, prayed, diligently studied the Bible, held overnight prayer meetings, circled cities, and flew over countries praying for revival. We hit the streets sharing our faith. We made sure our lives were holy so as to proclaim the gospel even further. When that didn't produce the mega results for which we longed, many of us doubled our efforts.

42

As time went by, and "revival" didn't come, we began to see it as a carrot perpetually dangled ahead of us which we could never obtain no matter how consistently we prayed, how holy we lived, or how diligently we served. It never dawned on us to ask, "Why?" We just kept plowing forward reaching for that promised prize not ever noticing the donkeys we'd become.

The problem was that we formulated a picture in our minds of what revival would look like, and we were looking for that image to be realized. If revival had walked up to us one day, shaken our hands, and said, "Hello, I am Revival," we would have likely not recognized Him and kept on the same futile course.

As you know, this is exactly what happened to the religious leaders when Jesus began to minister. For centuries, the Jews anticipated the coming of the Christ. God sent John the Baptist to prepare them to receive their Messiah, but they rejected John. God confirmed Christ's ministry by sending a dove at His baptism, turning water into wine, through His teachings which were like no other, by feeding thousands supernaturally, healing the multitudes, raising the dead, and by being raised from the dead; but they rejected Jesus. They rejected their own Messiah.

This is because the Scribes and Pharisees had a different expectation for the revival for which they longed, and Jesus did not fit the picture of the Messiah they anticipated. How could a Nazarene, born under questionable circumstances be the Messiah? Unthinkable! Besides, all the people were flocking to hear *Him*. This caused an understandable jealousy and was seen as a threat. They had labored diligently, lived holy lives, and along came this Jesus who was neither Scribe nor Pharisee, leading the people away from *them*. They were reasonably perturbed. Because of this, they missed the day of their visitation. They not only *missed* Him, their own Messiah, they saw to it that He was crucified. Then they proceeded to persecute, threaten, and sought to eradicate those who believed in Him all the while convinced they were doing the will of God.

Historically, we see that the religious establishment commonly sought to suppress the truth of the gospel beginning with the Scribes and Pharisees who persecuted Jesus and the Early Church, followed by the Judaizers in the region of Galatia who tried to muddy the waters by adding law to grace. Over the centuries, constant attempts have been made to modify the gospel, and those who sought to revive the original pure gospel were seen as a menace.

In the latter 1960's and early 1970's there was a revival among the Baby Boomers. My husband and I were at the tail end of this awakening. It was our joy to proclaim that being a Christian was not the religion many of us had criticized. It wasn't about do's and don'ts. Being a Christian was a *relationship* with Jesus Christ. All of us were glowing with this joy, so happy to know God, to be close to Him, and to sense His love and presence daily in our lives. Over time, though, this relationship we once celebrated morphed into mostly systematic religious practices.

Those who saw this happening spoke up against this fall from grace, but were usually greeted with distain and dismissed as "antinomian" or "extreme".

It's always easier to ignore someone we have labeled.

It might have been easy for us to miss or dismiss the call for doctrinal purity 20 or 30 years ago, but it seems impossible to me that this could be accomplished today. Any minister who has not noticed what is happening right now within the body of Christ truly has his head in the sand and his fingers in his ears or lives in a location devoid of communication. **All over the world voices are rising up, and even though their teachings may vary slightly, we cannot deny the common thread among them—a clear call to return to the pure gospel of God's amazing grace.**

Grace!

That used to be such a wonderful word among all believers, and yet now it is becoming a controversy—something some are even "sick and tired" of hearing. Imagine that! The grace of God—*disdained* and *controversial!*

44

Yet was not Jesus, who was "full of grace and truth", seen as controversial as He lived upon this earth? Was not His name upon the critical lips of the religious leaders and all the people as they maliciously plotted to get rid of Him? After His death and resurrection, the preaching of the cross was considered foolishness and offensive. Who were those who were *most* offended and who shunned, despised, and persecuted the message of the cross? It was the religious establishment.

Brothers and sisters, I implore you to please consider this fact. **We are the religious establishment of our day.** All of those "in ministry" within the Body of Christ could be compared to the Scribes and Pharisees. We've studied. We've labored. We've fasted and prayed and worked to see revival. We've lived exemplary lives and wanted nothing more than to please God. Some of us have parents and grandparents who have done the same. No one has been as diligent as we, to study, to give ourselves, to sacrifice our lives in the service of God and others, often without being appreciated, sometimes even treated with unkindness and cruelty. **Beloved, if we are not the religious establishment, then there isn't one.** Is it possible that with all of our knowledge and religious pedigree we could miss the very thing for which our hearts have been crying out?

Grace! God's amazing grace!

One little word, yet so powerful! **Are we missing it by *dismissing* it?** Do we seek to "balance" it with other things, such as law or works thus nullifying its power? Do we give it a polite nod for a few weeks of sermons and then move on to what we consider "deeper" truths? Are some of us even guilty of trying to snuff it out?

It is extremely important to know whether or not we are unknowingly fighting against the true gospel of God's grace.

The problem with any deception is that those believing it are deceived and don't know it. Could it be that we, the church, are *deceived*?

We know that Saul fought against the church in the extreme; not only trying to persuade people that this new sect was certainly not of God, but by delivering its followers to be put to death! Why would he do this? Was he an evil murderous person? No. It was because Saul truly believed that this new sect was a threat to *God* Himself. He felt he was doing God's will by persecuting these traitors who dared to say that righteousness came only through believing in this Jesus and not by obedience to the law of Moses which he deeply believed in and so diligently followed. Imagine his rage. Faith in a fake Messiah! Faith in His cross! Faith in His resurrection! It offended him to the very core of his existence. Yet, we know, that Saul was unknowingly deceived.

Does this sound at all familiar? Could it even happen today—that God would send messengers to declare again the message of the cross and *we* would actually fight against it—against Christ Himself? Doing so would be even worse than the Scribes and Pharisees because we are born again. Shall we now persecute our own brothers and sisters in Christ? Would we really despise His grace?

Grace! God's unlimited and unmerited favor!

Perhaps if we saw it as "error" we would feel it is the *responsible* thing to do to argue against it theologically as did the Judaizers in the early church. So, the Sunday morning sermons would begin to confront this "new" theology by giving a more "balanced" approach to grace.[5] Thinking that people are being "deceived" by such teachings and attempting to isolate and silence those teaching grace, we might even label them as "antinomians" or "grace extremists" or sideline what God is doing among us as simply a "Christian fad".

Is the *grace* of God a *fad?* Is it?

What if that isn't effective? What if this so-called "hypergrace" doctrine keeps "spreading like a *cancer*"? How far would we go to extinguish it? Would we move from these somewhat civilized responses to something more cynical? Would we ask those teaching it to "find a place of worship

---

[5] Can grace be "balanced? As our daughter, Joella, puts it, "Grace cannot be balanced. Grace is entirely unbalanced—in our favor."

more in line with their beliefs"—in essence throwing them out of the "synagogue"? Would we begin to make false accusations based on half-truths against these voices in order to defame them and thus shut them up? Would we warn people to "be careful" with whom they "associate" after we've given these "grace extremists" the left foot of fellowship? Would we cast aspersions on their character behind their backs? Would we even resort to violence?

My brothers and sisters, these things are already happening.

This is a very important question which deserves our sincerest consideration. What if the church—what if *we*—are actually fighting against the very revival we've been asking God to send? What if *this* is the day of our visitation? Will we refuse to hear as did the Scribes and Pharisees? Will we, as Saul did, persecute the church of God even Christ Himself?

The multitudes were flocking to Jesus. They were *hearing* what He had to say. The Scribes and Pharisees were not pleased. They were endeavoring to undermine His message—attempting to catch Him in His words, finding fault according to the law. Imagine healing someone on the Sabbath day or claiming to forgive sins without a sacrifice!

People by the thousands are beginning to return to the pure message of the gospel of the grace of God, delighted and overjoyed to rediscover that God really loves them and that what He did in Christ is more wonderful, more amazing, more marvelous than they ever realized and as beautiful as they once hoped and believed. They are breaking free from a religious system that has kept them bound under a myriad of laws and expectations and are beginning to enjoy their relationship with God once again. Yet, not everyone is sharing in their delight. What is being revealed to them is being met with skepticism even opposition by others. Just as with Jesus and with every other reformation, the most resistant to authentic revival has been the religious establishment.

When I say "authentic" revival I am referring to the exact meaning of the word itself—to bring *back* to life something that used to be alive, but now is dead or dying. Take a drowning victim, for example. When the lifeguard gives CPR, he is attempting to "revive" the person. The church *does* need to be revived, but not in the way we traditionally think of it. While one of the eventual outcomes of authentic revival is the forsaking of sin, forsaking sin does not bring revival. **At its core, true revival has to do with restoring life.** In order for the church to experience this much needed resuscitation it must once again receive the pure message of God's grace. Thus, authentic revival is what it's always been—a call to return to the pure gospel of the grace of God which rejects the notion that something more than faith in His grace is required in order to be saved and live the Christian life.

Reading these words can be disorienting, even irritating, **but is it not worth our sincerest consideration in light of our church history?** What if the church *today* is in error as it has been repeatedly over the centuries? Shouldn't we want to *know*? Isn't it worth a moment or two of our time and serious consideration? Isn't the truth the point? Of course, we want the truth. David and I longed for truth with all of our hearts and sought to love God and please Him in every word and deed. We thought we *were* teaching the truth. We were giving our lives to bring Him glory, doing everything we knew to serve Him. We thought we were doing what was right or we would not have been doing it at all.

Regrettably, we were *wrong*. In all of our zealous love for God, my husband and I missed the core message of the gospel, that not only are we saved by God's grace alone through faith in Christ alone, but that when Jesus said, "It is finished," He meant it.

48

Day 4

ADDING TO THE GOSPEL

---

*M*y parents' water supply came from a well, fed by an underground spring. When David and I would make the three hour drive to visit them, long before the popularity of drinking bottled water; we used to bring bottles to fill up so that we could take this fresh water home. They had an unlimited supply and were happy to share with us. What I would give to once again drink from that well!

There is nothing so clean tasting and satisfying as water like this. However, if to a glass of this clean, sparkling, and refreshing water, you were to add anything else, say a spoonful of poison, you would have sense enough not to drink it.

Yet, what if that spoonful of poison was added one itsy bitsy dissolving grain at a time? One little speck would probably not even be detected. How about two? Probably not. Over the years, you might not notice that what you were drinking was no longer fresh water. When it began to make you ill, would you even think to question the water you'd always enjoyed—the water your own parents were giving you?[6] Not likely. You might even drink more of it believing it would help you feel better.

The gospel of Jesus is like perfect, clear, flowing spring

---

[6]   By no means am I questioning the good motivations of parents or spiritual leaders. I am simply making the point that when the source is trusted, we drink without fear.

water. Just as a fresh glass of water from a spring delights a thirsty body, we once drank from the living water of God. Not only did we drink, but as Jesus promised, rivers of living water flowed from our innermost being. We knew the delight of our new birth and the realization that we had become the very children of God! We longed to learn all we could to equip ourselves to be the best Christians we could be so that we might please God in every word, deed, and thought and share our joy with others. As long as our teachers did not stray into what we considered cultic theology, we embraced what they taught. Our pastors were honest, upright, and sincere people so we trusted them to teach us the truth. We believed everything they said. We filled up multiple notebooks while taking meticulous notes. We were diligent to incorporate what we were taught into our daily living, not wanting to be like those who heard the word but did not do it.

Here's what we didn't think to consider during those years. What if the truths we were hearing and applying *weren't* completely true? What if our very upstanding pastors had been incorrectly taught? These thoughts never occurred to us because we *believed* in them. In our minds, these men wanted nothing more than to help us to be successful and productive Christians; to guide us so that we could avert the possibility that we would ever fall back into sin. These goals were noble and good. On top of that, for us to question what they taught would not only put in doubt their moral fiber, but it would be to "touch God's anointed". So, little by little, one tiny morsel at a time, the fresh spring of truth was poisoned, and we became ill, never perceiving why.

My husband and I marvel at the way we lived in fear of disagreeing with our pastors. We did not think it necessary to "prove all things and hold fast to that which is good" when it came to what *they* taught. We were taught to walk in "unity" and never ever say or do anything that would in any way "harm" the pastors. We wouldn't have imagined doing such a thing for we loved them so deeply and were determined to be the type of people in whom our leaders could trust. We feared the very retribution of God if we made one little peep. So we were extremely careful to keep any questions and criticisms to ourselves—even to vanquish them from our thinking. However, our blind trust and underlying fears, facilitated our gradual deception.

Perhaps, as we did, you felt the tug of the Spirit calling you to a life of service, and you responded. You studied. You lived a holy life and gained experience formulating your beliefs and your perception of what the Christian life is and what it requires. What if you were also ill-informed along the way? Could it be that you, like we, embraced "truths" that are not true?

Day 5

BY GRACE THROUGH FAITH NOT LAW

Galatians 2:21
*I do not **set aside the grace of God**; for if righteousness comes through the law, then Christ died **in vain**."*

*I*t isn't that we do not understand the basic tenants of Christianity, but that we have added to them. This is exactly what the teachers in Galatia were doing.

The "other" gospel about which Paul was warning the Galatians wasn't a cult like we would define it in our day. The Judaizers taught the same Jesus that you and I embrace. They believed that Jesus came in the flesh and rose bodily. They believed He was God. The Galatians were born again believers not converts to a cult who had never been regenerated. They believed what we all believe; that we are saved by grace through faith, not by works, and that this salvation is a *gift* from God. So, why was Paul upset with them? **Why did he pronounce a curse on anyone preaching "another" *gospel* if they were already saved?** Why did he say he wished their false teachers would go all the way and castrate themselves? Why was he so furious?

Our problem in discerning the answer to these questions has two core causes. First of all, as do the cults, we redefine terms. For example, we read "law" and translate it "ceremonial and civil law" automatically omitting the moral aspect of the law of Moses. By doing so, we miss the import, not only of the message of Galatians, but of all the teachings of Paul.[7]

The second reason for our blindness about why Paul was so unyielding about what was taught comes from not clearly understanding that the gospel is not exclusively for the lost *before* salvation but also for Christians afterward. The gospel is everything that pertains to the initial, continued, and ultimate salvation of *believers*. Paul knew the Galatians were believers. He addressed them as such. **If the gospel is only for non-believers, then why would Paul be so upset that *believers* had embraced "another" *gospel*?** The answer is clear: Paul didn't see the good news as a message for the unsaved only; rather, he saw it as the sum of what he taught; his very ministry.

Acts 20:17-24

*From Miletus he sent to Ephesus and called for the **elders** of the church. ¹⁸ And when they had come to him, he said to them: "You know, from the first day that I came to Asia, in what manner I always lived among you, ¹⁹ serving the Lord with all humility, with many tears and trials which happened to me by the plotting of the Jews; ²⁰ **how I kept back nothing that was helpful, but proclaimed it to you, and taught you publicly and from house to house**, ²¹ testifying to Jews, and also to Greeks, **repentance toward God and faith toward our Lord Jesus Christ.** ²² And see, now I go bound in the spirit to Jerusalem, not knowing the things that will happen to me there, ²³ except that the Holy Spirit testifies in every city, saying that chains and tribulations await me. ²⁴ **But none of these things move me; nor do I count my life dear to myself, so that I may finish my race with joy, and the ministry which I received from the Lord Jesus, to testify to the gospel***

---

[7] I write about the moral law in more detail in Chapter 13.

of the grace of God. ²⁵ *"And indeed, now I know that you all, among whom I have gone **preaching the kingdom of God**, will see my face no more.* ²⁶ *Therefore I testify to you this day that I am innocent of the blood of all men.* ²⁷ *For I have not shunned to declare to you **the whole counsel of God**.*

The "**gospel** of the **grace** of God" is what Paul taught, and the gospel of the grace of God *is* the whole counsel of God. It was his "race" and "ministry" given to him from Jesus Christ. He taught it day and night. Grace—for years. Grace, grace, and more grace. It wasn't a topic he addressed now and then and after that continued to the "deeper" things of God. The gospel of the grace of God *is* the glad tidings of good things; **grace *is* the deeper things of God**, and he preached it to believers as well as non-believers daily, publicly, and from house to house.

In his letter to the Galatians, again and again, Paul expresses law as *opposed* to grace, and most concur; no one is saved by law, not even the moral law. Yet, the Galatians were already born again by grace through faith and not law. We get to the core of what is really disturbing Paul when we read Galatians 3:1-3.

*O foolish Galatians! Who has bewitched you that you should not **obey the truth**, before whose eyes Jesus Christ was clearly portrayed among you as crucified?* ² *This only I want to learn from you: Did you receive the Spirit by the **works of the law**, or by the hearing of faith?* ³ *Are you so foolish? **Having begun in the Spirit, are you now being made perfect by the flesh**?*

"Begun in the Spirit" refers to their initial salvation. Paul wasn't concerned about their perception of how they were born again. He was warning them about a "gospel" that taught that subsequent to salvation they could be made *perfect* by the flesh.

"Being made perfect" is *epiteleo* which means "to bring something to the place where it is complete."[8] Without any stretch we can rephrase Paul's question, "Are you so foolish, having begun in the Spirit, are you now being made complete by your own human efforts?"

This is concluding, of course, that Paul was assuming that they *needed* to be perfected. The possibility that he was actually reprimanding the Galatians for thinking that they *needed* to be perfected at all, should also be considered. This question is relevant because Hebrews 10:14 proclaims that by one sacrifice He "perfected forever" those who are sanctified. If we are "perfected" (teleioo) *forever*, perhaps the Galatians' folly was thinking they *needed* to be perfected (epiteleo) at all. At first glance this seems a viable interpretation. However, we can't ignore Philippians 1:6 where Paul wrote, "being confident of this very thing, that He who has begun a good work in you will complete (epiteleo) it until the day of Jesus Christ".

What are we to conclude? Are we perfected or are we not? What did Paul mean when he said that Jesus would complete the work He started in us?

As we focus on the context of Hebrews 10, we see that the author states that we have been "perfected forever" by the one sacrifice offered for our sin. This forgiveness of sin resulted in our salvation. Through that offering Jesus perfected us forever in the sense that our sins are forever forgiven and our redemption is sure. Wuest confirms this understanding.

*The word "perfected" is the translation of **teleioo** which means "to bring to a state of completion." Here, the completeness of the state of salvation of the believer is in view. Everything essential to the salvation of the individual is included in the gift of salvation which the sinner receives by faith in Messiah's sacrifice. The words "for ever" here are to be construed*

---

[8] Wuest's Word Studies–Wuest's Word Studies – Volume 1: Word Studies in the Greek New Testament

with "perfected." It is a permanent state of complete-
ness in salvation to which reference is made. The
words "them that are sanctified" are descriptive of the
believer. He is one set apart for God.[9]

Using Hebrews 10:14 and Philippians 1:6 we can conclude that we are both perfected (*telieoo*) in regard to everything Jesus accomplished on the cross, *and* subsequently brought to a state of completion (*epiteleio*), which most certainly refers to our maturation, or one might say, to fulfilling what Jesus already accomplished. This would include aspects such as being transformed by the renewing of our mind (Rom. 12:2) and from glory to glory by beholding Jesus (2 Cor. 3:18). We aren't born again knowing every right from wrong, but grace teaches us to forsake worldly lusts and to live godly (Ti. 2:12). The fruit of the Spirit grows (Gal. 5:22). Our character develops (Rom. 5:3-4). We become rooted and grounded in God's love (Eph. 3:17). Our understanding and appreciation of what was accomplished through Jesus' life, death, and resurrection becomes clearer to us (2 Tim. 3:16-17). Our discernment between good and evil matures (Heb. 5:14).

Let me put it this way. Everything that Scripture teaches was accomplished by Christ's death is "finished." Yet, there is a process of our current perfection being brought to completion from beginning to end. **What is essential to understand is that it is *Jesus* who brings to completion this work that He started—not we through our own efforts.** This growth comes by the working of the Holy Spirit in our lives.

Let's look again at Paul's question in order to understand this in closer detail. In what ways were they trying to complete themselves?

---

[9] Wuest's Word Studies–Wuest's Word Studies – Volume 2: Word Studies in the Greek New Testament

*This only I want to learn from you: Did you receive
the **Spirit** by the **works of the law**, or by the hearing
of **faith**? [3] Are you so foolish? Having begun in the
Spirit, are you now being made perfect by the **flesh**?*

Notice that Paul is coupling the Spirit with faith, and the
works of the law with the flesh. Thus, I offer this paraphrase,
"Are you so foolish, having been born again by the **Spirit** of
God—by grace through **faith**, are you now being brought to
completion by the **flesh—the works of the law—through
your own efforts** (instead of by grace through faith)?"

Here is where we can connect with Paul's concern; where
the modern-day church can hear the Holy Spirit's plea. For
we agree wholeheartedly with our beloved brother Paul that
we are born again by simply believing in Christ's resurrection
and confessing Jesus as Lord, but do we stray just as the
Galatians did about the manner in which we are perfected
after salvation? Do we sing that He who started the good work
in us "will be faithful to complete it,"[10] and then work diligently
at completing it *ourselves*? Do we preach the *good* news that
we are saved by grace through faith to the lost, but deliver
a completely different "gospel" to the saved—one which is
perceived by millions of believers today as something closer
to *bad* news? **Are we giving the very clear message that
after we are graciously saved apart from works, we then
must begin a regimen of works in order to maintain and
improve upon our relationship with God?**

These questions are very important to consider, for if we
teach believers that it is by *their* discipline that they are perfected after salvation instead of by grace through faith—the
Spirit, then clearly we are preaching "another" gospel; the
very "gospel" upon which Paul pronounces a curse for those
who teach it.

On the contrary, we are saved by grace alone through
faith alone. **Our further perfection/completion is as much**

---

[10] "He Who Began a Good Work in You" by John Mohr, © 1987 Birdwing
Music

a miracle as our salvation. As we walk in this grace, we grow. Notice, He does the work.

Colossians 2:6-7
As you *therefore have* ***received*** *Christ Jesus the Lord,* ***so walk*** *in Him,[7] rooted and built up* ***in Him*** *and* ***established in the faith****, as you have been taught, abounding in* ***it*** *with thanksgiving.*
Galatians 5:25
If we live in the Spirit, let us also ***walk*** *in the Spirit.*
1 Thessalonians 5:23-24
Now may the God of peace ***Himself*** *sanctify you completely; and may your whole spirit, soul, and body be* ***preserved*** *blameless at the coming of our Lord Jesus Christ.* [24] *He who calls you is faithful,* ***who also will do it****.*

Day 6

THE GIFT OF RIGHTEOUSNESS

*U*nder the Old Covenant, righteousness was based on keeping the law. Under the New, it is a *gift* from God by faith in Jesus, purchased for us by His blood.

Philippians 3:7-10
*But what things were gain to me (my religious pedigree and obedience to the law—see the preceding verses), these I have counted loss for Christ. ⁸ Yet indeed I also count all things loss for the excellence of the knowledge of Christ Jesus my Lord, for whom I have suffered the loss of all things,¹¹ and count them as rubbish, that I may gain Christ ⁹ and be found in Him, **not having my own righteousness, which is from the law, but that which is through faith in Christ, the righteousness which is from God by faith.***

---

[11] Traditionally, it has been taught that the things which Paul counted as rubbish and forsook were the sins of his past and worldly pleasures and that we would be wise to follow his lead. On the contrary, he was not referring to anything unlawful in his life, rather how well he kept the law and how godly he lived! Are we able to tell our congregations to forsake following the law as a means of righteousness and seek the righteousness that comes by faith?

We *know* we are righteous by faith at *salvation*, but the perception of most believers is that *after* salvation we are righteous by means of not sinning and by doing what is right. **We need to see that this way of "living" is what Jesus Christ died to *change*.**

Righteousness derived from refraining from sin, doing works, and practicing spiritual disciplines is nothing less than *self*-righteousness (v 9).

The problem with self-righteousness (law-based righteousness) is it is inadequate. What if someone (a non-believer) were very disciplined and motivated and able to live a perfect life; never sinning and *always* doing *everything* from pure motives and for the good of others; loving God with *all* of his heart, and *all* of his strength, and in *every* thought, word, and deed—even giving most of his fortune to help the needy? Would that person be righteous before God under the New Covenant? Absolutely not! We know and are persuaded that no one apart from Christ will stand before God and declare that he is righteous, even if he is perfect in *every* way, even if he *never* sinned because all are *born* unrighteous. Before Christ, we are sinners in need of righteousness. We are dead in need of life. The *only* way sinful man can be righteous and come alive is through faith in Jesus Christ.

Romans 5:12-17

Therefore, just as through one man sin entered the world, and death through sin, and thus death spread to all men, because all sinned— [13] *For until the law sin was in the world, but sin is not imputed when there is no law.* [14] *Nevertheless death reigned from Adam to Moses, even over those who had not sinned according to the likeness of the transgression of Adam, who is a type of Him who was to come.* [15] *But the free gift is not like the offense.* **For if by the one man's offense many died, much more the grace of God and the gift by the grace of the one Man, Jesus Christ, abounded to many.**

*[16] And the **gift** is not like that which came through the one who sinned. For the judgment which came from one offense resulted in condemnation, but the **free gift** which came from many offenses resulted in **justification**. [17] For if by the one man's offense death reigned through the one, much more **those who receive abundance of grace and of the gift of righteousness will reign in life (in life will be reigning) through the One, Jesus Christ.***

Righteousness, the righteousness of God, is a **gift**. It can never be earned under the New Covenant, before salvation or after. **On the contrary; we are not righteous *by* living righteously, we live righteously *because* we have been *given* righteousness.**

We have missed this glorious truth almost entirely though some of us might be able to express it doctrinally. This fact is most clearly evidenced by the constant call from the pulpit to "get right with God", especially in youth groups. What we are saying when we make this plea is that those listening are *not* right with God because they sinned or because they haven't been doing enough good, and that in order "to *get* right with God" they need to stop sinning or begin to do more of what is good—and there is always more good that one can do making it impossible to do enough. This throws our religion back to righteousness derived by keeping laws—and we become guilty of preaching the very "other" gospel about which Paul expressed his deepest concern.

This amazing *gift* of righteousness seems too good to be true, so we redefine terms to make it more palatable. We say, "We are *positionally* righteous, but in actuality we are not righteous unless we *live* righteously." Any way we express it, as soon as we base our righteousness on obedience; either to do what is "right" or to not do what is "wrong",[12] we are placing ourselves and those who hear us under religious law. We are

---

[12] I put "right" and "wrong" in quotes because these standards vary from church to church.

compelling them to endlessly attempt to perfect themselves in the flesh (in their own strength) which is a futile effort.

Under the New Covenant, righteousness—perfect right-standing before God, is and can only ever be a *gift* because it was purchased *for* us by the sacrifice of Jesus Christ and cannot be merited. We are not only righteous by faith in the sense that Abraham was righteous (because he believed God and thus righteousness was imputed to him), we have been *made* the very righteousness of *God* through the offering of Christ!

> ***2 Corinthians 5:21*** *Mounce*
> *He made him who knew no sin to be a sin-offering for us, so that in him we might become the righteousness of God.*

Hear this! We *are* righteous *apart* from religious law. If we aren't then Jesus Christ was rejected and falsely accused, despised and beaten, crucified and spilled out all of His precious blood for no purpose!!! We need to see that when we pervert the *gift* of righteousness into something that is *developed* by our *own* efforts, the flesh, we are robbing from *Him* what *He* did for us. We are saying that what He did was insufficient—that He was only able to give us a "standing" but not an "actual" righteousness.

> ***Galatians 2:21*** *Amplified*
> *[Therefore, I do not treat God's gracious gift[13] as something of minor importance and defeat its very purpose]; I do not set aside and invalidate and frustrate and nullify the grace (unmerited favor) of God. For if justification (righteousness, acquittal from guilt) comes through [observing the ritual of] the Law, then Christ (the Messiah) died groundlessly and to no purpose and in vain. [His death was then wholly superfluous.]*

---

[13] What gift? The gift of righteousness.

The law is good. God made the law, and what He makes is perfect. However, the law of Moses had a precise purpose for a specific people and for a limited time. It was never meant to be permanent. It was given *until* Jesus would die, but after Jesus died and faith in Christ came, the law was no longer necessary for those who believe.

Galatians 3:21-25

*What purpose then does the law serve? It was added because of transgressions, **till** the Seed should come to whom the promise was made; and it was appointed through angels by the hand of a mediator. [20] Now a mediator does not mediate for one only, but God is one. [21] Is the law then against the promises of God? Certainly not! For **if** there had been a law given which could have given life, truly righteousness would have been by the law. [22] **But** the Scripture has confined all under sin, **that the promise by faith in Jesus Christ might be given to those who believe.** [23] But **before faith** came, we were kept under guard by the **law**, kept for the faith which would afterward be revealed. [24] Therefore the law was our tutor to **bring** us to Christ, that we might be **justified by faith**. [25] **But after faith has come, we are no longer under a tutor.***

How we missed verse 25 for so many years still baffles us. In fact, just the other day, when we quoted it to a friend to show that we are no longer under the law, someone who has been a Christian nearly as long as have we, he replied, "That's not in the Bible—is it?" Yet it is crystal clear to us now. We no longer need a tutor for the law has been replaced by grace, our new teacher.

Titus 2:11-14

*For the **grace** of God that brings salvation has appeared to all men, [12] **teaching us** that, denying ungodliness and worldly lusts, we should live soberly,*

*righteously, and godly in the present age, [13] looking for
the blessed hope and glorious appearing of our great
God and Savior Jesus Christ, [14] who gave Himself
for us, that **He** might redeem us from **every** lawless
deed and purify for Himself His own special people,
zealous for good works.*

The law was never meant for those who receive righteousness as a gift by faith, but for sinners. In other words,
the law *does* serve a purpose, but not in the life of a believer;
not for the righteous.

1 Timothy 1:8-11
*But we know that the law is good **if** one uses it
lawfully,[14] [9] knowing this: that the law is **not made
for a righteous person**, but for the lawless and
insubordinate, for the ungodly and for sinners,[15] for
the unholy and profane, for murderers of fathers and
murderers of mothers, for manslayers, [10] for fornica-
tors, for sodomites, for kidnappers, for liars, for per-
jurers, and if there is any other thing that is contrary
to sound doctrine, [11] according to the glorious gospel
of the blessed God which was committed to my trust.*

Beloved, the law is not made for us. We are the righ-
teousness of God apart from the law. We are the righteous.
Faith has come! We have no need of a tutor. Under the New
Covenant God writes His law in our hearts; not the law of
Moses, the Old Covenant law, but the New Covenant law of
Christ.[16] We no longer need to be told to "know the Lord".
We know Him. All believers know Him, from the one who
was born again yesterday to those who have followed Him
for decades; from the child who has faith in Him to the oldest

---

[14] Amplified: "for the purpose for which it was designed."
[15] Notice that Paul is making a distinction between a righteous person
and a sinner. He is contrasting a believer with a non-believer.
[16] Gal. 6:2

among us; from the least esteemed to the most honored. We *all* know Him apart from the law because of what *He* did, His grace, and our faith in Him.

> ***Jeremiah 31:31-34***
> *"Behold, the days are coming, says the Lord, when I will make a* ***new*** *covenant with the house of Israel and with the house of Judah—* [32] ***not*** *according to the covenant that I made with their fathers in the day that I took them by the hand to lead them out of the land of Egypt, My covenant which they broke, though I was a husband to them, says the Lord.* [33] *But this is the covenant that I will make with the house of Israel after those days, says the Lord: I will* ***put My law in their minds, and write it on their hearts****; and I will be their God, and they shall be My people.* [34] ***No more*** *shall every man teach his neighbor, and every man his brother, saying, 'Know the Lord,'* ***for they all shall know Me, from the least of them to the greatest of them****, says the Lord.* ***For*** *I will forgive their iniquity, and their sin I will remember* ***no more****."*

Yet how many sermons have we heard and taught that emphasize "knowing" the Lord? Dear ones, the day we received Jesus by faith, we knew the Lord. Yes, we can learn more *about* Him and our experience with Him obviously increases, but we all already know Him and He knows us. To send a saint on an endless journey to obtain something that has already been given in Christ is to negate what Jesus accomplished *for* us through His death and to plunge God's people into needless despair.

So then, "another" gospel can be simply defined as adding religious requirements (obedience to laws) to grace and faith in order to maintain or improve (perfect) ourselves.

What an astonishing realization was ours when we saw that almost everything we taught, that is being taught in churches, and that is written in countless

Christian books today *is* **about how to maintain or improve our relationship with God!**

Because we, the church, perceive "the gospel" as only being for the lost, we hesitate to preach the "*glad* tidings of *good* things" to the saved. We don't teach them that they *are* the righteousness of God; we scold them for not living righteously. We keep insisting that we are still sinners, when the truth is we are the righteous, and we scoff at those who teach otherwise. We fear that if we affirm our right-standing with God, our righteousness, some might run off helter-skelter and live like the unrighteous. We think it is our *responsibility* to continually point out short-comings and call for repentance. Then we prescribe a self-improvement plan which includes not sinning and doing such things as praying more, reading the Bible more, reading this book or that one, or attending a conference.

We teach these religious requirements for righteousness with confidence because they are the same ones that were taught to us and the ones our teachers were taught by their teachers who learned them from their own teachers and on and on. **However "spiritual" these practices seem to be, however mainstream, however "good", when we begin to see them as** *why* **we are righteous before God as believers and as a means to preserve or build upon what Jesus accomplished by His death and resurrection, they become nothing more than an expression of self-righteousness.** They are self-perfection, the flesh—"another" gospel.

Romans 5:19
For as by one man's disobedience many were made ***sinners***, *so also by* ***one*** *Man's obedience many will be made* ***righteous***.

Day 7

NO MORE

*M*ost of my Christian life I perceived that I was right with God based on the manner in which I lived my life and never once considered that this was the exact definition of self-righteousness.

One need only search for a new believer manual in the nearest Christian bookstore to discover that the very minimum disciplines each believer "needs" to practice in order to preserve and enhance his relationship with God (beyond refraining from sin) are to pray and read the Bible daily.[17] Initially, these exercises begin out of relationship. We know God and feel close to Him, so we pray. We want to learn more about Him, so we study. How easily and quickly we pervert these motivations born out of love into making prayer and Bible study a *requirement* to the extent that someone not regularly practicing "spiritual disciplines" feels he must *repent* of not practicing them! Do we really believe that if someone is not having daily devotions he is *sinning*?

How my husband and I would have answered that question many years ago is evidenced by how many times we repented of not praying "enough".

Secondly, and even more ingrained in our thinking, is the belief that when we sin (not in the sense of "omission" but of

---

[17] We all know that "the list" is much longer than simply praying and reading the Bible, but just to simplify, I'm only addressing these two.

"commission"), we are no longer righteous. We are taught that this can take on varying consequences from incurring God's displeasure, "breaking fellowship" with God, being "separated from God", to even deserving His wrath. We're told that if we incur His displeasure He'll refuse to hear our prayers, and if we are separated from Him by our sin, He *can't* hear our prayers. Others go further and intimate that God's blessings will be hindered in our lives (the windows of heaven will be shut); or even worse, that we will "open the door for Satan" to wreak havoc in our lives. Not until we confess and forsake our sins will we be forgiven for sin and protected from the devil, we are falsely told; some even adding that if the trumpet sounds before this confession takes place or if one dies suddenly while sinning he will be left behind and even perhaps be eternally lost.

What this produces is millions of Christians, young and old alike, living in insecurity and paranoia instead of confidence and peace. Many end up confessing sins all day long horrified they might forget something they did, said, or thought that doesn't quite measure up to perfection. They end up constantly thinking about sin. Logically, if the Lord might return any moment, one is best not to wait until one's next prayer time to "take care of things", they surmise. Think of this. Christians, children of a loving God, who gave His only Son to *take away* our sins are living each day in fear of perhaps forgetting to confess one of them. In fear of their Father! In fear of Satan! In fear of being eternally damned!

Is this good news? No, it is not. Yet, this is what is being taught to God's own beloved children.

Romans 8:15

For you did not receive the spirit of bondage again to fear,[18] but you received the Spirit of adoption by whom we cry out, "Abba, Father."

---

[18] In context, this "spirit of bondage" is the law.

How can anyone be at peace with God and have a one-on-one loving relationship with Him with no barriers if he thinks God is holding something against him? Do you have someone in your life who refuses to forgive you? How is your relationship with that person? I'm pretty sure it is not what you wish it could be. In fact, it might be the source of much sorrow and agony. Perhaps you've apologized again and again, but your sins are still being held against you. You might not even know why the person is upset with you because they won't talk to you about it. You feel helpless to do anything to fix it. Or, you've been forgiven by him in the past, but now you have to walk on egg shells when you are around him for fear you might once again fall out of this person's favor. You can never be yourself, never relax, never feel loved, and never enjoy being around him.

Friends, this is a reflection of how many people feel about their relationship with God. Yes, they were forgiven initially, but now that they are God's children, they don't ever quite feel "clear" with Him, and that sense of total forgiveness before God and the joy it brought is mostly a memory now. In their minds, He has become distant and indifferent toward them, and some people have no idea what they did to deserve God's cold shoulder. What they need to know is that God has completely and forever forgiven us, and He is not keeping any records. He's not angry with us. He isn't waiting for us to "get it together" before He'll pour out His love upon us. We walk righteous and holy before Him because of the blood of Jesus. Without this knowledge a person cannot be at peace with God.

"Get right with God or else!" Perhaps you haven't heard this additional grave news, but we were told by teachers that visited our church (information that was never denied after they left) that God is like some Big Brother constantly videotaping our lives and that at the Judgment Seat of Christ every rotten thought or word or deed we ever committed after becoming a Christian will be displayed for all to see.[19] We might still be saved from eternal damnation, but we can be sure, it is claimed, that God will make us suffer for our sin by humiliating us before all of our brothers and sisters in Christ.

We have to compartmentalize this type of thinking because it goes against what Scripture teaches us. Will the God who says, "Love covers a multitude of sins," expose them to all?

When we believe these things, our focus becomes overwhelmingly on sin and what *we* must do about sin instead of understanding and teaching the good news: that we *are* forgiven of *all* sin.

Colossians 2:13
*And you, being dead in your trespasses and the uncircumcision of your flesh, He has made alive together with Him, having forgiven you **ALL** trespasses.*

We are forgiven! How complicated we have made this glorious truth when it is so gloriously simple and wonderful. Jesus Christ came to *save* us from our sins.

Matthew 1:21
*And she will bring forth a Son, and you shall call His name JESUS, for He will **save His people from their sins**."*

Forgiveness is not a clean-slate process in which only our past sins are removed. We are *saved* from our sins—*all* of our sins!

He shed His blood to not only forgive us, but to set us free from sin's power. We preachers think this freedom will come to those who hear us because we emphasize law. If we don't tell people right from wrong, we worry, how will they

---

[19] Our son, Tim, points out the following. "Imagine the torture and horror, not just for the person being exposed but for all of us being forced to watch triple X-rated videos for perhaps many years!!!"

know? The glorious truth is that the law is not what liberates us from the power of sin; rather, it is His grace.

Romans 6:14
*For sin shall not have dominion over you, **for** you are **not** under law but under **grace**.*

In fact, the law actually strengthens sin. Yes, you read that correctly.

1 Corinthians 15:56
*The sting of death is sin, and **the strength (dunamis) of sin is the law**.*

Jesus became a sin offering for us so that we could be forgiven and set free from sin. We preach this good news to the lost, and they receive it with joy. Oh, the wonder of knowing one's past sins are forgiven and forgotten simply by putting our faith in Jesus as the Lord! However, we don't preach the same gospel to believers, God's beloved children. Instead, we teach a *conditional* forgiveness. What a disappointment is ours when we "discover" that while we were His enemies He forgave all of our sins by grace through faith, but now that we are His children, there is a different standard—right standing by law through works.

How forgiven are we as believers? Completely and forever.

Hebrews 10:1-18
*For **the law**, having a shadow of the good things to come, and not the very image of the things, **can never** with these same sacrifices, which they offer **continually** year by year, **make those who approach perfect**. (Keep in mind that the writer of Hebrews is contrasting the law system of forgiveness with the forgiveness Jesus would provide.) [2] For then would they not have **ceased** to be offered?*

For the worshipers, once purified, would have had
no more consciousness of sins. ³ *But in those*
sacrifices there is a reminder of sins every year.
⁴ *For it is not possible that the blood of bulls and*
goats could take away sins.
⁵ *Therefore, when He came into the world, He said:*
"Sacrifice and offering You did not desire,
But a body You have prepared for Me.
⁶ *In burnt offerings and sacrifices for sin*
You had no pleasure.
⁷ *Then I said, 'Behold, I have come—*
In the volume of the book it is written of Me—
To do Your will, O God.'"
⁸ *Previously saying, "Sacrifice and offering, burnt*
offerings, and offerings for sin You did not desire,
nor had pleasure in them" (which are offered
according to the law), ⁹ *then He said, "Behold, I have*
come to do Your will, O God." He takes away the
first that He may establish the second. (This is
referring to taking away the Old Covenant system
and establishing the New.) ¹⁰ *By that will we have*
been sanctified (been made holy) through the
offering of the body of Jesus Christ once for all.
(Did you hear that? We were MADE HOLY once for
all.) ¹¹ *And every priest stands ministering daily and*
offering repeatedly the same sacrifices, which can
never take away sins. ¹² *But this Man, after He had*
offered one sacrifice for sins forever, sat down at
the right hand of God, ¹³ *from that time waiting till His*
enemies are made His footstool.

¹⁴ *For by one offering He has perfected forever*
*those who are being sanctified.*²⁰

---

²⁰ This is referring to those who are being saved. NASB reads, "those
who are sanctified".

¹⁵ But the Holy Spirit also witnesses to us; for after He had said before,
¹⁶ "This is the covenant that I will make with them after those days, says the Lord: I will put My laws into their hearts, and in their minds I will write them,"
*¹⁷ then He adds, "**Their sins and their lawless deeds I will remember no more.**" ¹⁸ Now where there is remission of these, **there is no longer an offering for sin**.*

For many years, David and I failed to understand the intent and import of verse 14. The Amplified version translates it this way.

For by a single offering He has forever completely cleansed and perfected those who are consecrated and made holy.

Now, wouldn't that be good news; to know that by *His* one offering we are forever and completely cleansed and perfected and consecrated and made holy (sanctified)? Not just initially, but completely and forever?

The writer of the letter to the Hebrews, possibly knowing that this amazing news might fly over the heads of its recipients, gives another witness, that of the Holy Spirit, quoting from Jeremiah 31:31-34. Now, we grasp that Jesus was the last offering for sin, but what many of us miss is that God is *no longer* remembering our sin—not just our past sin, but *all* of our sin: past, present, and future.

I don't expect you to accept this truth immediately, so let us also hear what Paul writes in Romans 4:5-8.

*But to him who does **not** work but **believes** on Him who justifies the ungodly, his **faith** is accounted for righteousness, ⁶ just as David also describes the blessedness of the man to whom God **imputes** righteousness **apart from works**:*

⁷ *"Blessed are those whose lawless deeds are for-*
given and whose sins are covered;
⁸ *Blessed is the man to whom the Lord* **shall not**
impute sin. *"*

"Impute" means to take an inventory or to credit to one's
account. Beloved, God is not imputing sin to us. We are the
ones about whom David prophesied. God is *not* crediting us
with sin. He's not keeping a record of our wrongs. Our sins
are forgiven and we are being continually cleansed from all
sin. That's how powerful His blood is in our lives!

1 John 1:7
But if we walk in the light as He is in the light (if
we are born again), we have fellowship with one
another (only those in Christ have fellowship with
each other), and the blood of Jesus Christ His Son
*cleanses (**is cleansing**)²¹ us from all (all, any, every,*
the whole) sin.

This is the good news, the gospel that needs to be
preached to believers: We are forgiven completely and
continually.
His Son's sacrifice was not like the Old Covenant sacrifices which could never make the worshippers perfect. His
sacrifice was more than adequate, so very complete that
now we can enjoy what the law could never give: freedom
from the very consciousness of sin!

Hebrews 10:1-2
*For **the law**, having a shadow of the good things to*
*come, and not the very image of the things, **can never***
*with these same sacrifices, which they offer **con-***
tinually** year by year, **make those who approach

---

²¹ The Amplified reads, "and the blood of Jesus Christ His Son cleanses
(removes) us from all sin and guilt [keeps us cleansed from sin in all its
forms and manifestations]."

__perfect__. ² For then would they not have ceased to be offered? For the worshipers, once purified, would have had __no more consciousness of sins__.

At first we are tempted to put up our defenses, but please hear what the Holy Spirit is saying in these passages. The law constantly condemned the people. It showed them their faults, but could not change them. The worshippers offered the sacrifices for forgiveness but they always came back again for more forgiveness. This need for repeated forgiveness was because they had not been made perfect because the sacrifices of the law were *not good enough*. The worshippers still possessed a sin-consciousness.

As my beloved husband often asks, "Was Jesus' sacrifice good enough?" Or is there something we need to add to it? If it is good enough, then we should no longer have a consciousness of sin.

Romans 8:1-4

There is therefore now no condemnation (negative sentence for sin)²² to those who are in Christ Jesus, who do not walk according to the flesh, but according to the Spirit. ² __For the law of the Spirit of life in Christ Jesus has made me free from the law of sin and death.__²³ ³ For what the __law could not do__ in that it was __weak__ through the flesh, __God did by sending His own Son__ in the likeness of sinful flesh, on account of sin: He condemned sin in the flesh,

---

²² *Condemnation* has often been used to describe guilt or shame, but it is much more than a feeling. Condemnation refers to a negative consequence, such as a sentencing in a court of law. A murderer might be *condemned* to life in prison, for example. What Paul is declaring is that Jesus has set us free from being condemned/sentenced/judged, for sin. Jesus said, "Most assuredly, I say to you, he who hears My word and **believes in Him** who sent Me has everlasting life, and shall **not come into judgment**, but has passed from death into life," (John 5:24).

²³ The Law of Moses; see also Acts 15.

*⁴ that the righteous requirement of the law might be fulfilled in us who do not walk according to the flesh but according to the Spirit.*²⁴

Please don't misunderstand what I'm saying. **These scriptures are not saying that we no longer have a conscience. They aren't saying we no longer have a sense of morality.** In fact, we know that the conscience of a believer is more acute than that of a non-believer because we are new creations. What the author is saying is that the law was not good *enough* to free the believer from *sin*-consciousness—the bondage of always feeling guilty and thus condemned.

Consider the person who is all day long confessing every sin; guilty and horrified that he might have "unconfessed" sin. Is this not the quintessential manifestation of sin-consciousness? This person can never know true peace with God because he believes that *he* must focus on getting his sins forgiven.

Friends, Jesus' offering *was* good enough. It was sufficient to remove all sin from us forever. His sacrifice doesn't have to be offered repeatedly through endless confession of sins. Our sins are already forgiven and God remembers them no more due to his *one time* sacrifice. He is not keeping a record. There is no video. Glory to God forevermore!

Does this good news seem too good? Read on.

The priests never sat down while they were making offerings for sins because there were always more sins to "get under the blood". Jesus, however, "sat down". He said, "It is *finished.*" The price for sin and our sanctification was paid once and for all. Our sins are forgiven forever. All of our sins are *already* removed by His blood; we don't need to put them there.²⁵ We can now stop focusing on our sin—being sin-con-

---

²⁴ Paul is NOT equating those who "walk in the flesh and not in the Spirit" to believers who sometimes do what is wrong and those who sometimes do what is right. See Chapter 26 for a more complete explanation.

²⁵ There is NO scripture instructing us to "put our sins under the blood". This is tradition based on a misunderstanding of the New Covenant.

scious, and begin to be **Jesus**-conscious, living in praise and worship for the One who offered up His own body to set us *free* from sin and sin-consciousness. Instead of focusing on getting forgiveness, we can direct our energies toward loving each other and doing the works which God "prepared beforehand that we should walk in them" (Eph. 2:10).

There is no space in time after we sin that we are *not* forgiven. This is why we are never separated from God when we sin and why no door is opened for Satan; for during the very act of sinning, we are already cleansed. Completely and forever. He no longer remembers our sins. He is not imputing (accounting) them to us.

Does the knowledge that we are forgiven, even in the act of sinning give us a desire to sin? God forbid!

No stronger illustration of this good news can be found than Paul's admonishment *against* sexual sin.

1 Corinthians 6:13b-20
*Now the body is not for sexual immorality but for the Lord, and the Lord for the body. [14] And God both raised up the Lord and will also raise us up by His power. [15] Do you not know that your bodies are members of Christ? Shall I then take the members of Christ and make them members of a harlot? Certainly not! [16] Or do you not know that he who is joined to a harlot is one body with her? For "the two," He says, "shall become one flesh." [17] But he who is joined to the Lord is one spirit with Him. [18] Flee sexual immorality. Every sin that a man does is outside the body, but he who commits sexual immorality sins against his own body. [19] **Or do you not know that your body is the temple of the Holy Spirit who is in you**, whom you have from God, and you are not your own? [20] For you were bought at a price; therefore glorify God in your body and in your spirit, which are God's.*

The horror that Paul was describing to the Corinthians who were involved in sexual immorality was *not* that it would separate them from God or open a door for Satan. There is no mention of such a thing. Instead, Paul reasons with them, not based on the fear of separation from God; on the contrary, but on the basis that we are one Spirit with Him. He demonstrates that *they were taking the Holy Spirit with them when they were engaging in sexually immoral activities.*

The Holy Spirit is in us and abides with us forever (Jn.14:16) and Jesus promised to never ever leave us or forsake us, not ever (Heb. 13:5). Neither one of those passages adds exceptions.

So, it is not that God might be imputing our sin against us that should bring us dismay, or the fear that if we sin, the devil will have some right to harm us, and certainly not that we might go to hell, but that since we are the temple of the Holy Spirit we are bringing God with us into whatever immorality we are doing. The one committing sexual immorality is doing so in the very presence of the Father whose Son is advocating for him and whose blood is cleansing him from all sin.

This amazing grace (truly here, his *unmerited* favor), this immense *love*, is what should turn us away from sin, not the fear that God will broadcast it to all. When we sin, God still loves us through Christ. He truly remembers our sins no more. Knowing this and believing it, does not set us free to sin, but sets us free to not sin and releases our hearts to worship.

Romans 4:8 Amplified
Blessed and happy and to be envied is the person of whose sin the Lord will take no account nor reckon it against him.

Day 8

WHAT ABOUT 1 JOHN 1:9?

*E*very Bible teacher understands how easy it is to misinterpret Scripture by lifting one verse out of its context and developing a doctrine around it. Most work diligently toward not being guilty of doing this when we prepare a teaching.

Yet, the church *has* done this with 1 John 1:9. It has become the core of our understanding of how it is we are forgiven of sin now that we are believers. We make many conclusions based on this *one* verse setting aside the clear evidence within 1 John and in the whole of the New Testament Scripture that we are forever and continually cleansed by the one-time sacrifice of the blood of Jesus. We don't need to *seek* forgiveness. We are already forgiven. Let's look at this again.

Hebrews 10:11-14 NASB
Every priest stands daily ministering and offering **time after time** *the same sacrifices, which can* **never take away** *sins; [12] but He, having offered* **one** *sacrifice for sins for* **all time**, *sat down at the right hand of God, [13] waiting from that time onward until His enemies be made a footstool for His feet. [14] For by* **one offering** *He has* **perfected for all time** *those who are sanctified.*

Animal sacrifices offered by fallible priests were unable to "take away" sin, and they could not make the worshippers holy. That's why forgiveness under the law had to be obtained again and again. When Jesus atoned for sin, however, He atoned *one* time for *all* sin, taking away our sins—forever making us perfect in regard to sin. There is no other sacrifice for sin. *We* can do nothing to obtain forgiveness. It is already ours.

However, we ignore this information when reading 1 John 1:9. The first false assumption made is that while Jesus provided forgiveness through His blood, this forgiveness is not automatic, but must be *obtained*. The second notion is the formula itself: that if we sin, we *must* confess our sins *in order* to be forgiven and cleansed of that particular sin. Then come the conclusions based on these false assumptions: that if we *don't* confess our sins, we are *not* forgiven and that if we are not forgiven, we are obviously not right with God until we confess our sins; many adding that in this state we could end up in hell!

However, as my husband often points out, 1 John 1:9 must itself be interpreted by Scripture and not Scripture by 1 John 1:9.

For many years I resisted what I am about to write and with good reason. 1 John 1:9 was a sacred practice for me most of my life. I'd been taught that when I sinned, I could go to the Father and confess my sins and be not only forgiven but cleansed of all unrighteousness (in that area, I would add in my mind). In my thinking, this was a freedom I enjoyed as a believer in Jesus Christ. I could go *directly* to God and ask for forgiveness unlike *other* religions that taught one had to go to a spiritual leader in order to obtain forgiveness. I had *direct* access for forgiveness. I practiced 1 John 1:9 so many times, that I cherished this formula. It "worked" for me, so it had to be true, I thought. I found comfort in *doing* something to gain forgiveness. I saw it as *my* part in the equation. In my mind I was truly trusting in the blood of Jesus to forgive me. I didn't think that confession alone provided forgiveness. I didn't believe for one moment that I was doing any more than obeying the method I had been taught. I didn't understand, because no one ever taught me, that **I was already forgiven and that this continual confession, even with the understanding that only by His blood could I be forgiven, was not necessary.** What I could not see because I was blinded by the tradition I held, was that the first chapter of 1 John was written primarily as a testimony to *non-believers.* I fought this idea because 1 John 1:9 was my personal holy tradition passed down to me from all those who taught me. How could so many people be wrong? Now before going into automatic convulsions about the topic as I used to do, please hear me out.

One evening as I sat in my office I opened my Bible and, as we'd done with so many treasured topics over the years since we woke up to His grace, bowed my head and said, "Lord, I just don't get what people are saying about 1 John 1:9. If I am missing something, please show me personally." What happened next surprised me and shook me to the core! I honestly did not expect to see *anything* I had not seen previously, but there it was in plain sight. John was *witnessing* to sinners not instructing believers. Formerly, I had only been able to conclude that "we" and "us" were used to include the intended audience which I thought to be Christian. Suddenly I saw that "we" and "us" were the ones testifying to "you", those who did not yet believe.

1 John 1:1-8[26]

That which was from the beginning (attesting to His deity), which we[27] *have heard, which we have seen with our eyes, which we have looked upon, and **our hands have handled**, (affirming that John personally could testify that Jesus, prior to and after His resurrection, had a body and was not a spirit*

---

[26] As with all quotations from the NKJV, comments within parenthesis not found in the original text are added for clarification.

[27] "We" refers to those who heard and saw and touched Jesus.

being) concerning the Word of life— ² the life was manifested, and we (those who walked with Him personally) have seen, and bear witness, and declare to you (to those of you who don't know or who still doubt) that eternal life which was with the Father and was manifested to us (those who believe)— ³ that which we (those who believe) have seen and heard (Jesus) we declare to you, (John is preaching the gospel to the lost) **that you also may have fellowship with us;** *(those whom John is addressing this chapter did NOT have fellowship with them yet because they were not yet born again) and truly our fellowship (speaking of himself and those who were also believers with him) is with the Father and with His Son Jesus Christ (attesting that he and those with him were believers). ⁴ And these things we write to you that your joy may be full. (Our joy is full. We know the Savior. We want you to know Him so you may have the same joy.)*

Suddenly, I saw it clearly: John is addressing non-believers[28] in Chapter One, but let us continue.

⁵ This is the message which we have heard from Him and declare to you (those of you who do not know the message), that God is light and in Him is no darkness at all (John is attesting to God's perfect character and holiness). ⁶ If we say that we have fellowship with Him (if we say we are born again), and walk in darkness, we lie and do not practice the truth (those to whom he was speaking were walking in darkness—not saved. If someone claims to be a Christian, and is walking in darkness, that person is a liar.) ⁷ But if we walk in the light as He is in the

---

[28] It is important to note that John does not address *believers* until chapter two unlike 2ⁿᵈ and 3ʳᵈ John where he immediately identifies his audience as believers.

*light (if we are Christians), we have fellowship with one another (only believers have fellowship with each other), and the blood of Jesus Christ His Son cleanses (is cleansing) us (believers) from all (ALL) sin. ⁸ If we say that we have no sin, we deceive ourselves, and the truth is not in us (he is implying that some among them, the **unbelievers** whom he is addressing, were saying they had no sin).*

We know and trust that faith in the real Jesus is essential to salvation. Some have written that John is addressing *believers* who did not believe Jesus came as a human being, and yet he goes on to say later in his letter that if we do not believe that Jesus came in the flesh we are not saved. So, anyone holding this view could not be a believer.

1 John 4:1-3
*Beloved, do not believe every spirit, but test the spirits, whether they are of God; because many false prophets have gone out into the world. ² By this you know the Spirit of God: **Every spirit that confesses that Jesus Christ has come in the flesh is of God, ³ and every spirit that does not confess that Jesus Christ has come in the flesh is not of God**. And this is the spirit of the Antichrist, which you have heard was coming, and is now already in the world.*

We also know from verse eight that the people John is addressing are not believers because the truth is not in them. It reads, "If we say that we have no sin, we deceive ourselves, and the truth is not in us." If the truth is not in someone, that person is not a believer.

Then we read verse nine, the solution to *unredeemed* man who does not think he has sin. "If you confess your sins," that is to say, if you "agree with God" that you have sin, "He is faithful and just to forgive us our sins and to cleanse us from *all* unrighteousness." This describes initial salvation perfectly. We are forgiven of sin and cleansed of *all* unrighteousness, so much so that we are made the very righteousness of God (2 Cor. 5:21).

While belief in and confession of the risen Jesus as the Lord is what is essential to salvation, it is clear to all that redemption/salvation includes forgiveness of sin. John's audience denied their need for forgiveness, even that they had sin. What I'm saying is that even though confessing sins formally is not a *prerequisite* for salvation (Rom. 10:9-10); the awareness that we need and receive forgiveness is certainly present since Jesus died to save us from our sins.

Since I understood this truth, I've read substantiating arguments about this from writers more eloquent and detailed than I, but in my opinion the strongest argument goes back to basic hermeneutic principles. **We must not use one verse to form a doctrine, but must allow the verse to be interpreted by its context and the whole of Scripture.**

So, let us consider the following very important information about the historical context. John wrote 1 John around 90 AD, long after Paul died; obviously after all of his letters were written; letters which form our understanding of the gospel. **It is of weighty significance to note that while Paul did correct believers about their behavior, he never once expressed in any of his letters that a believer needed to confess his sins in order to be forgiven.** Instead, he always affirmed that our sins are already forgiven—all of them. If it is essential for us to confess our sins *in order* to be forgiven and cleansed, then why did Paul not include this crucial information in at least one of his letters (if not in all of them)?

How irresponsible it would have been for Paul to not mention such a crucial formula! By not doing so, he would have condemned all of his followers to having thousands of sins that were not "put under the blood". Surely, he would have brought it up in Romans 6, that great chapter about our freedom from sin. Why didn't he say, "You are free from sin, and you can get further forgiveness when you confess your sins"? Shouldn't he have expressed the formula of confession leading to forgiveness and cleansing to the erring Corinthians? He didn't discuss it because he didn't believe it to be necessary. Paul spoke of sin as something that is *already* forgiven.

Ephesians 1:7
*In Him we **have** redemption **through His blood**, the **forgiveness** of sins, according to the riches of His grace.*

Colossians 2:13-14
*And you, being dead in your trespasses and the uncircumcision of your flesh, He has made alive together with Him, **having forgiven you ALL trespasses**, [14] having wiped out the handwriting of requirements that was against us, which was contrary to us. And He has taken it out of the way, having nailed it to the cross.*

Paul reasons with his readers to walk worthy of what they had already been given. He reminds them that since they are forgiven of *all* trespasses and are seated with Christ, to set their minds on heavenly things not earthly. Because they already died, were hidden in Christ, and raised with Him, they should not sin. When Christ appeared, they would appear with Him in glory because of what Jesus did. Paul never taught that believers needed to confess every sin to get forgiveness because he viewed believers as already forgiven.

Ephesians 4:1
*I, **therefore**, the prisoner of the Lord, beseech you to walk worthy of the calling with which you were called.*

Colossians 3:1-4
*If then you were raised with Christ, seek those things which are above, where Christ is, sitting at the right hand of God. [2] Set your mind on things above, not on things on the earth. [3] **For you died, and your life is hidden with Christ in God**. [4] When Christ who*

is our life appears, then you also will appear with Him in glory.

Then there is the proof within John's first letter. When he clearly is addressing the believers in chapter two, he affirms that they are already forgiven.

1 John 2:12
*I write to you, little children, because your sins **are** forgiven you for His name's sake.*

Then, later in his letter, he has something very different to say about a believer who sins than what we assume he is saying in 1 John 1:9. There is no formula, only a statement of fact.

1 John 2:1
*My little children, these things I write to you, so that you may **not sin**. And **if anyone sins, we have an Advocate with the Father, Jesus Christ the righteous**.*

This is very important to notice. John *does not say*, "If anyone sins, simply confess your sin and you will be forgiven and cleansed." He says to the *believer*, "If you sin, you have an Advocate." Our Advocate's blood is cleansing us continually from ALL sin. Read it one more time.

1 John 1:7
*But if we walk in the light as He is in the light we have fellowship with one another and the blood of Jesus Christ His Son cleanses (is cleansing) us from **all** sin.*

We have been forgiven for **all** sin. If we sin we are cleansed, not because we confess to get forgiveness, but because our Advocate, Jesus Christ, already paid the penalty for all of our sins, which at the time He died were all in the future. His blood reached across our entire lifetime and across all of history. That's how complete His sacrifice was.

Now, some will agree that according to 1 John 1:7 His blood continually cleanses us from all sin, but then insist that 1 John 1:9 teaches us that we need to seek "relational" forgiveness with God (which in no way is indicated by the context of that chapter). This comes from the conclusion based on false assumptions that I mentioned above—the false belief that when we sin, our relationship with God is somehow strained, and for this reason, we must confess our sins in order for our relationship with God to be "restored". This idea cannot be substantiated based on the fact that "our sins and our lawless deeds He remembers no more". Our relationship with God is never in jeopardy.

Now of course, when we offend someone, we apologize. There is nothing wrong with expressing our regret to God for something we have thought or said or done; but not *in order* to be forgiven, and certain*ly* not *because* our relationship with Him needs mending. God does not sit offended and brooding when we sin. On the contrary, when we sin, His grace and compassion and love superabound to us, and He begins to work all things together for our good—yes, even our mistakes

Some of us, even understanding that we are perfectly forgiven forever, might hesitate to teach this glorious truth because we fear that the flock will run off and go on a sinning binge. Yet, this good news does not promote freedom *to* sin, rather, freedom *from* sin, so that the *opposite* of what we fear occurs in the heart of someone who truly understands His grace. When we realize that we are *forever* forgiven of *all* sin, we do not desire to sin, instead, our hearts rise up in worship!

If you doubt that teaching perfect forever forgiveness will result in less sin than more sin, reflect on the scene of the sinful woman who washed Jesus feet with her tears and dried them with her hair in the house of Simon (Lk. 7:36-50). He was disgusted that Jesus would allow such a sinner to touch Him. So, knowing his thoughts, Jesus told him a parable about two men, one who owed much and one who owed little who were both forgiven for every debt when they were unable to pay. Jesus then asked Simon, "Who do you think loved him more?" Simon correctly answered, "The one who was forgiven more."

Can you hear this? This woman, who was a sinner, was clearly the person who owed "much". Jesus knew that this woman was not going to go out that door and continue in her sin because she had a clean slate to fill again with sin. The joy of knowing she was forgiven completely would cause her to love Jesus all the more and cause her to forsake sin and this person was not even born again.

When we, those who have been born again, understand how greatly and completely we are forgiven, it doesn't cause us to love less, but more! It doesn't cause us to sin more, but rather to forsake sin.

Oh, the joy of peace with God; the clear understanding that nothing, not even sin can separate us from our Father's love!

Day 9

FREEDOM FROM SIN

---

1 Corinthians 15:1-4

*Moreover, brethren, I declare to you **the gospel which I preached to you**, which also you received and in which you stand, ² by which also you are saved, if you hold fast that word which I preached to you—unless you believed in vain.³ For I delivered to you first of all that which I also received: **that Christ died for our sins according to the Scriptures**, ⁴ and that He was buried, and that He rose again the third day according to the Scriptures.*

*N*otice first of all that the gospel Paul preached was that Jesus died for our sins. He died for *all* of our sins, and this is very good news for it is why and how we are saved (v 2). Not only is it how we are saved initially, but the Greek reads, "through which also you are *being* saved". Again, as I have shown previously, salvation and forgiveness are not only initial, but continual; thus the gospel is not only for the lost but for the saved.

Salvation is not some cheap "bait and switch" scheme whereby we happily proclaim to the lost that they can be saved and forgiven of their sins, but after they are born again they discover that salvation and forgiveness have to be maintained by their continual confession and right living; that their past is forgiven, but their future is always contingent upon something *they* must do, and they must confess each and every sin in order to even have the right to fellowship with God. God forbid it! The glad tidings of good things is not a momentary bliss later to be replaced with the continual consciousness of sin and the sense that our righteousness is based on our obedience and that even our salvation is in question.

There are so many Christians, who instead of feeling secure in their relationship with God live daily with a sense of insecurity—never sure whether they are "right" with God, if He is pleased with them, or if they have confessed enough sins to ensure their salvation.

The glad tidings of good things from our great God that we have been totally and forever forgiven, is not only how we are saved, but that in which we *stand* (v 1). Thus, the good news is not only for the lost but for us, the beloved children of God. What would happen in a church that focused on the good news of our certain salvation, our forever forgiveness, our blood-bought holiness, and God's glorious gift of righteousness, instead of constantly pointing out how hopelessly wretched we are followed by endless prescriptions for self-improvement?

Revival! Authentic revival.

We think that by preaching "hard" against sin, revival will break out, but actually, according to Scripture, the opposite is true. Shouting moral law at Christians does not set them free; it strengthens sin in their lives. Consider Prohibition which sought to externally stop the drinking of alcohol in the United States of America. Did it? No. In fact, by making drinking alcohol illegal, it was made more desirable. We think we are doing the right thing shouting, "Thou shalt not," and, "Thou shalt," but in actuality we are robbing from God's people what Jesus Christ *died* to give them: the *assurance* of eternal salvation, His very righteousness, and freedom from sin. This is because law strengthens sin. Paul makes this clear in verse 56 of this same chapter,

The sting of death is sin, and ***the strength (dunamis)***
of sin is the law.

Perhaps some among us might be so bold as to declare
this continual forgiveness, but would we be so bold as to
tell people that the *reason* they are free from sin is because
they are free from law?
"Not so fast!" we would warn, fearing the path of lawlessness. For if proclaiming we are completely and continually
forgiven doesn't cause believers to go on a sinning ram-
page; we think that certainly, teaching that we are not under
law will! Yet, that we are free from the law is so obvious,
David and I still wonder how we missed seeing it for so
many years.

Romans 6:14
For sin shall ***not*** *have dominion over you, for you are*
not under law *but under* ***grace.***

How amazing is His grace? It is the precise reason sin
does not have dominion over us.
Jesus didn't die so that we would be *able* to keep
the law. He died so that we could be *free* from it so
that we could live under grace which frees us from
sin's dominion.
We now know that one of the reasons we did not understand this glorious truth is because we tended to segment
our reading of certain passages of Scripture instead of perceiving the entire meaning in light of the context. An excellent example of this was that we saw the first few verses of
Romans 7 as a teaching on the permanence of marriage
instead of a continuation of chapter six and the information
needed to digest the rest of chapter seven. Read it again
with the understanding that we are delivered from and dead
to the law and not as a message about marriage.

Or do you not know, brethren (for I speak to those
who know the law), that the law has dominion over a

man as long as he lives? ² *For the woman who has a husband is bound by the law to her husband as long as he lives. But if the husband dies, she is released from the law of her husband.* ³ *So then if, while her husband lives, she marries another man, she will be called an adulteress; but if her husband dies, she is free from that law, so that she is no adulteress, though she has married another man.*²⁹ ⁴ **Therefore, my brethren, you also have become dead to the law through the body of Christ**, *that you may be married to another—to Him who was raised from the dead, that we should bear fruit to God.* ⁵ *For when we were in the flesh, the **sinful passions which were aroused by the law** were at work in our members to bear fruit to death.* ⁶ *But now **we have been delivered from the law**, having died to what we were held by, so that we should serve in the newness of the Spirit and not in the oldness of the letter.*

This could not be stated more clearly. We are dead to the law through the body of Christ. Prior to that, our sinful passions were aroused by the *law*. **Just to repeat that, law arouses sinful passions**. It doesn't diminish them. Now, however, we are delivered from the law. This death allows us to experience the joy of being freed from sin as described in Romans 6 and being alive to God as proclaimed in Romans 8.

If we don't teach this; if we insist that believers are still under law and that our right-standing with God is maintained or improved by keeping laws (the "dooties" and "don'ties" of "Christianity"), then we are preaching "another" gospel and making His sacrifice worthless or at best, provisional. As I

---

²⁹ At this point, one might think that Paul would declare that the law died and that is why we are free from it, but he gives us a supernatural twist. The law doesn't die, thus setting us free. We died in Christ to the law and are therefore free from it. We also see that the law and Jesus are put in opposition to each other.

have quoted before, "If righteousness comes through law, then Christ died in vain," (Gal. 2:21).

We must preach *the* gospel. This is what Paul is saying in Galatians. If we preach "another" gospel, we are accursed. Righteousness, right-standing with God, does not come through obedience to law. To teach this is to bring a curse upon oneself. Just that statement is difficult to write because the idea of saying such a thing, to me, seems over-the-top. I would have been the first to caution Paul against declaring something so severe! In my "civilized" live-and-let-live upbringing, it seems extreme. Why, Paul, do you have to be so unyielding about *what* is taught? Why can't you simply go with the flow when it comes to teaching? Why do you have to threaten teachers of the gospel? Why can't you just "walk in love and unity"?

Paul wrote with such boldness because he knew that the true gospel was being perverted, and he was fighting for its very survival. He cherished the gift of righteousness because it was purchased for us with the precious blood of his Savior. He bore in his body the proof that he suffered repeatedly for this truth.

If our righteousness is based on law, then Jesus did not need to die! He wasted his time on earth and His blood on the cross. Jesus did not die to help us get the ball rolling and now it's up to us. If Jesus died only to *empower* us to keep the law, instead of to set us free from it, He died for no reason. **Salvation is not the starting line for believers when it comes to sin and righteousness. It is the "It is finished!" line.**

Paul is not calmly telling us to consider our *manner* of preaching. He is imploring us to preach the one true gospel and not a *mixed* gospel based on grace plus keeping laws as a means of perfection. It is God's amazing grace that saves us and keeps us saved, not law. If you are preaching law-keeping as a means of continued righteousness, holiness, perfection or even as the way we now please God you might as well have spit on His beaten and bruised face as He hung dying on the cross to set us free from law!

It's not that we would do this deliberately. God forbid! Most of us are teaching as we were taught. Nonetheless, since many of us were taught incorrectly, we do well to consider these things. Whether deliberately or in ignorance, teaching "another" gospel brings misery to the hearers and those who do so are accursed.

Some of us shutter at the idea of teaching something different than what we were taught by those we love so deeply. It seems disrespectful to the memory of those who have gone before. Yet, do we seek to please men or God? If you want the praise of men, then go on preaching the same message that is being preached almost everywhere: that God saves us, but after that we have to maintain or improve our salvation by obedience and good works. No one within the church will persecute you for this. They will pat you on the back, in fact, and welcome you with open arms.

If you want the praise of God, then preach His radical gospel: that we were saved by God's grace through faith in Jesus, not by works, and this is exactly how we live this life. Teach that we began in the Spirit, and now we simply walk in the Spirit. Teach that our forgiveness is final and that God is not holding our sins against us at any time. Teach that we can KNOW 24/7/365 that we have eternal life. Teach that we are righteous apart from the works of the law. Proclaim that we are holy. You can rest assured that you will suffer persecution within the church for teaching such things.

Here is even more good news that we seldom hear. Jesus came to set us *free* from sin. Yet, do we really believe that we are free from sin? Romans 6 in its entirety is seldom taught; I believe, because its content is so radical. Imagine the Sunday sermon about how we are "dead to sin" as contrasted to the weekly sermons that *assume* we are controlled by sin.

Some use 1 John 1:8 to teach that it is wrong for believers to say they "*have* no sin"—that this would be untruthful, but the verse isn't speaking to believers at all but to non-believers who thought there was no such thing as sin. I've also heard this verse used to prove that believers *aren't* really *free* from sin, and for one to claim that we *are* free from sin *is* to sin! Are we to ignore, then, what Paul said in Romans 6 that we are dead to and free from sin? This is a severe error that contributes to the continued false belief that believers are the same as unbelievers in regard to sin and to sinning. Let me state this clearly. Sinners sin. It is their *nature* to sin. The righteous live righteously. It is our *nature* to live righteously. Believers are forgiven of all sin, dead to sin, set free from sin, and John states that he wrote his letter so that the reader would "not sin". If he is saying that believers "have sin" then he is contradicting himself in the same letter when he writes this shocking statement.

1 John 3:4-9

Whoever commits sin also commits lawlessness, and sin is lawlessness. ⁵ *And you know that* **He was manifested to take away our sins**, *and in Him there is no sin.* ⁶ **Whoever abides in Him does not sin**. *Whoever sins has neither seen Him nor known Him.* ⁷ *Little children, let no one deceive you.* **He who practices righteousness is righteous, just as He is righteous.** ⁸ *He who sins is of the devil, for the devil has sinned from the beginning. For this purpose the Son of God was manifested, that He might destroy the works of the devil.* ⁹ **Whoever has been born of God does not sin, for His seed remains in him; and he cannot sin, because he has been born of God.**

I have never heard a Sunday sermon on the above passage. It is one of the most stunning and amazing passages in Scripture! Is John out of his mind? Is he speaking in hyperbole? No. He is stating *truth*. Contrary to what is taught, the normal condition for a born again believer is to *not* sin. This makes some people very angry—to say that we don't sin, and usually 1 John 1:8 is used as evidence. **Of course we are *capable* of sin, just as were Adam and Eve *before* the fall, but it's not *normal* for new creations to sin.** In fact, the more we understand that we are forgiven, the less we desire to sin and the less we do sin. I've said this while teaching, and made a few people significantly upset with me, some even sure that I am lying through my teeth, but I seriously have no desire to sin. I don't struggle with sin, don't think about sin, and don't have to try really hard not to sin—in fact, the idea of possibly sinning saddens me, and if I do sin, I feel awful about it. I have a new nature. I am a new creation. I am holy and righteous. I am one spirit with the Lord. I am no longer a sinner. It is my new nature to *not* want to sin and to want to please God in every thought, word, and deed. **If you are a born again believer and this does not describe your life, my most educated opinion is that you are somehow living under law which is strengthening sin in your life.** The more we understand the grace of God and our total forgiveness of and freedom from sin, the less power it has in our lives.[30]

The good news is, we are forgiven perfectly and forever of all sin and marvelously set free from sin. This is the glorious reason that Jesus came and became a sin offering for us—to save us from our sins—to give us total and complete forgiveness and to make us the very righteousness of God (2 Cor. 5:21).

---

[30] If you are struggling with a particular sin or with a behavior that you want to eliminate, try this: Next time you are tempted, remind yourself that you are forgiven, that you are righteous, that you are holy, that God is with you, that He isn't condemning you, but loving you and working in you to set you free. Do this each and every time asking Him to help you see the freedom from sin that is yours. Study the Scriptures to see what He has accomplished in you. Reject the lie that you still have a sinful nature. (P.S. Contrary to certain translations, the terms "sinful nature" and "sinner" never apply to Christians.) Focus on the new creation He has made you. Thank Him that He is not holding your sins against you—that He is imputing to you His righteousness, not your sin. Reject the idea that you "can't" stop. Stop seeing sin as normal. It isn't. Embrace the freedom that is yours. Expect a supernatural change.

Romans 6:5-11

*For if we have been united together in the likeness of His death, certainly we also shall be in the likeness of His resurrection, [6] knowing this, that **our old man was crucified with Him**, that the body of sin might be **done away with**, that we should **no longer be slaves of sin**. [7] For he who has died has been **freed from sin**. [8] Now if we **died** with Christ, we believe that we shall also **live** with Him, [9] knowing that Christ, having been raised from the dead, dies no more. Death no longer has dominion over Him. [10] For the death that He died, He died to sin once for all; but the life that He lives, He lives to God. [11] **Likewise** you also, **reckon yourselves to be dead indeed to sin**, but **alive to God** in Christ Jesus our Lord.*

Day 10

THE BEGINNING AND THE END

*I*t is foundational to our understanding of whether or not we are teaching "another" gospel to discern where the Old Covenant begins and ends and where the New Covenant is inaugurated. Most ministers would be able to give the correct answers, but there are common misunderstandings about this topic among many believers today. Some think the Old Covenant began in Genesis, and vary on when they believe the New Covenant began. Some say it began at His birth; others say at His baptism or when He turned water into wine.

Part of our confusion arises from the traditional way in which Bibles are published. Immediately before the book of Genesis we find a page that reads, OLD TESTAMENT.[31] I'm sure it's not purposefully deceptive, but it gives the wrong impression about the Biblical timeline. We know that the Old Covenant did not begin until Moses was given the law. Prior to that time the Old Covenant did not exist.

It's interesting to note that prior to the giving of the Old Covenant, even though death reigned because of Adam's sin, there was an amazing lack of punishment for sin.

---

[31] Testament = Covenant

Romans 5:12-14

*Therefore, just as through one man sin entered the world, and death through sin, and thus death spread to all men, because all sinned— ¹³ (For until the law sin was in the world, **but sin is not imputed when there is no law**. ¹⁴ Nevertheless death reigned from Adam to Moses, even over those who had not sinned according to the likeness of the transgression of Adam, who is a type of Him who was to come.*

Cain, even though he killed his brother, did not receive the consequence he would have received under the law— death. Instead, God put a mark on Cain that was meant to *protect* him against receiving retribution from others for what he'd done (Gen. 4:15). Think about that, God protected the first murderer!

Before the flood, "the wickedness of man was great in the earth, and every intent of the thoughts of his heart was only evil continually," (Gen. 6:5). For hundreds of years this went on with few consequences. To curb this trend, the lengthy lifetime mankind enjoyed was shortened from multiple hundreds of years to only 120 years. However, man's behavior continued to deteriorate and God repented of having made him.[32] Man was hopelessly evil, and yet, "Noah found *grace* in the eyes of the Lord."

Noah believed God and built the ark, but his behavior, while certainly not as debased as those who lived around him, was not always pristine. After this amazing experience of hearing God's voice in so much detail that he was able to build an ark capable of carrying hundreds of animals and surviving a storm worse than any in history, after having been a "preacher of righteousness", after living through the destruction of almost all of mankind and yet being saved,

---

[32] Some speculate that fallen angels had joined themselves physically with women on the earth (Gen. 6:1-4), and if God had not destroyed them all, there would have been no pure human left to bear the Messiah "when the fullness of time had come".

and receiving the promise that God would no longer flood the earth, we find that this grace was unmerited after all. He planted a vineyard, made wine, got drunk and uncovered himself in his tent. Was Noah punished or even rebuked for his behavior? No; rather, his sons were commended for covering his nakedness instead of exposing it, and Canaan, the son of Ham who revealed his shameful behavior, was cursed.

Let us also consider Abraham who was told to leave his family behind and relocate in Canaan, but instead he allowed his nephew, Lot, to travel with him (Gen. 12). Although having Lot under his care turned out to be a nuisance for Abraham, God did not rebuke him for his disobedience nor retract his choice to make of Abraham a nation. Abraham also married his half-sister, which the law, when it came, would forbid (Lev. 18:9), yet God chose to bring Isaac from their union. Abraham went along with his wife's idea to sleep with her mistress to bring about God's promises, yet even the fruit of his union with Hagar, this "mistake", was given a blessing by God (Gen. 17:20).

We know, too, that Abraham misrepresented (lied) to Pharaoh and King Abimelech about his relationship with Sarah to save his own life and allowed her to be taken into a harem![33]

Was Abraham reprimanded by God for any of this? No. In fact, those who took Sarah were the ones whom God rebuked and cursed even though they had acted on false information. Abimelech was even told to have Abraham pray for him so the curses on them would be removed. Did Abraham suffer any consequence as a result of his deception and betrayal? No. Astonishingly, Abraham received from the ones he'd deceived an abundance of their riches instead.

I say all of this to point out that first of all, the Old Testament does not begin in Genesis and that before the giving of the law, God dealt with those He called with an amazing amount of mercy and grace. Even the three months

---

[33] Gen. 12, 20

after Israel was delivered from Egypt, the people enjoyed much grace. Consider that before the Covenant came, their grumblings were met with undeserved provision (Ex. 16-17). After the giving of the Law, their complaints were met with judgment (Num. 11, 14, 16).

We have a similar and slightly more complicated confusion with the page in our Bibles entitled, "NEW TESTAMENT", for clearly the New Testament did not begin at Jesus' birth, but at His death.

Hebrews 9:16-17
*For where there is a testament, there must also of necessity be the **death of the testator**. [17] For a testament is in force after men are dead, since **it has no power at all while the testator lives**.*

Jesus was born under that law and His ministry and teachings were primarily to those under the law. While He was on earth, the Old Covenant was still in place. Not until Jesus became a sin offering for mankind did the New Covenant begin. When the New began, the Old was nullified.

Galatians 4:4-5
*But when the fullness of the time had come, God sent forth His Son, born of a woman, **born under the law**, [5] to redeem those who were under the law, that we might receive the adoption as sons.*

Why is this significant? It is important because it helps us rightly divide (accurately handle) the Scripture which is *all* given by inspiration of God, and it is especially helpful when considering the import of the words of Christ.

Here is an excellent example my husband recently pointed out to me.

Luke 10:25-28

*And behold, a certain lawyer stood up and tested Him, saying, "Teacher, what shall I do **to inherit eternal life**?"*
*[26] He said to him, "**What is written in the law**? What is your reading of it?"*
[27] So he answered and said, "'You shall love the Lord your God with all your heart, with all your soul, with all your strength, and with all your mind,' and 'your neighbor as yourself.'"
*[28] And He said to him, "You have answered rightly; **do this and you will live**."*

I will discuss this topic more thoroughly in Chapter 24, but let me ask you this. If someone were to ask us today **how to inherit eternal life**, is this the answer *we* would give? Love God completely and love others? Of course, not! Hopefully, we would tell someone who wants to be born again to believe in the resurrection of Jesus and confess Him as the Lord God. So, how do we understand these words of Jesus that seem to contradict Romans 10:9-10? In context, of course. Jesus is talking to someone who is still under the Old Covenant. The question was specifically about *what is written in the law*. These two verses encapsulate the law and prophets. It was right for Jesus to tell this man to "do this and live" because the man was still under the law.[34]

This is not to say that the words of Jesus are irrelevant for New Covenant believers today as some have hinted, but that we need to recognize that some of what Jesus taught was meant to prepare the Jews for the kingdom of God and doesn't apply to us directly. Other things He taught are universally true in either covenant. Many things He said could not be understood even by His own disciples until *after* He

---

[34] The law was this man's tutor to bring him to Christ. It was right for Jesus to point to the law. He knew it would bring the man to faith in Jesus. Then after faith came, he would no longer be under the tutelage of the law (Gal. 3:23-24).

was crucified and had risen from the dead. Part of what He taught has little or nothing to do with us, especially when it concerned fulfilling the rituals of the Jewish law. Just as with any scripture, when considering the words spoken by Jesus, we must always keep in mind that when He walked on the earth, the Old Covenant was still in place, that Jesus was announcing the upcoming kingdom of God to the Jews, and that the New Covenant was yet to come. On this side of the cross, the kingdom of God has come.

Nor should we disregard what we call "The Old Testament" for there is much to learn from these writers. Yet it is imperative we view all of these passages in their context since not all of them directly speak to us but many were written to a specific people for a particular purpose. Of course, the most beautiful thing we can observe when we read Genesis through Malachi are the many passages which pointed to Jesus and the New Covenant.

Luke 5:39
You search the Scriptures, for in them you think you have eternal life; and these are they which testify of Me.

The Scribes and Pharisees knew the Scriptures, but they failed to see that Jesus was revealed in them.

Nor should we disregard the gospels though they occurred mostly while the Old Covenant was in place. One of the most glorious beauties we can behold within the gospels is an amazing understanding of God the Father. Consider this revelation that Jesus spoke to Phillip.

John 14:7-11
"If you had known Me, you would have known My Father also; and from now on you know Him and have seen Him."
[8] Philip said to Him, "Lord, show us the Father, and it is sufficient for us."

⁹ Jesus said to him, "Have I been with you so long, and yet you have not known Me, Philip? He who has seen Me has seen the Father; so how can you say, 'Show us the Father'? ¹⁰ Do you not believe that I am in the Father, and the Father in Me? The words that I speak to you I do not speak on My own authority; but the Father who dwells in Me does the works. ¹¹ Believe Me that I am in the Father and the Father in Me, or else believe Me for the sake of the works themselves.

Jesus was saying that to see Him was to see the Father. Paul makes this crystal clear in Colossians 1:15-20.

He is the image of the invisible God, the firstborn over all creation. ¹⁶ For by Him all things were created that are in heaven and that are on earth, visible and invisible, whether thrones or dominions or principalities or powers. All things were created through Him and for Him. ¹⁷ And He is before all things, and in Him all things consist. ¹⁸ And He is the head of the body, the church, who is the beginning, the firstborn from the dead, that in all things He may have the preeminence.¹⁹ For it pleased the Father that in Him all the fullness should dwell, ²⁰ and by Him to reconcile all things to Himself, by Him, whether things on earth or things in heaven, having made peace through the blood of His cross.

When we read the gospels, we not only learn from His words, but we get a glorious view of God the Father. Many Christians today have such a lovely view of Jesus, but then an entirely different view of our Father. Yet, Jesus is the visible image of the invisible God. God sent His Son, not only to die for us, but so that we could "see" Him. I believe this is the most wonderful thing we can take away from the gospels, to see the Father for who He is as He reveals Himself through the Son. We can see how He loves, what angers Him, what touches His heart, how He has compassion on sinners, and how He loves us so very much that He gave His only Son to die to save us. When we see Jesus in the Gospels, we see the Father.

It is only when we discover the dividing line between the Old and New Covenants that we are able to perceive the significance of the teachings of Christ and put them in their proper context. We must not assume that what Jesus spoke to an individual Jew applies directly to born again believers, but rather perceive the context and thus better appreciate and understand what is being said.

There is a clear dividing line between the Old and the New, and that line was drawn with His blood.

Day 11

OUT WITH THE OLD

---

*I*t is embarrassing to admit that for fifteen years my husband and I did not see the importance of understanding that the New Covenant is distinct from the Old. Let me restate that, just in case you are as dull in your thinking as we were. The New Covenant is different. It is not the same. The Old Covenant is old. The New Covenant is new. God didn't say, "This is the *additional* covenant I make with you," nor did He say, "Combine these two covenants." He said, "This is the New, *not* like the Old." Hopefully, your head is not as hard as ours were.

> ### Jeremiah 31:31-32
> *"Behold, the days are coming, says the Lord, when I will make a **new** covenant with the house of Israel and with the house of Judah— ³² **not** according to the covenant that I made with their fathers in the day that I took them by the hand to lead them out of the land of Egypt, My covenant which they broke, though I was a husband to them, says the Lord.*

God wants us as believers in Jesus Christ to understand that we are under the New Covenant only and not the Old because the New Covenant and its promises are better.

Hebrews 8:6
*But now He has obtained a more excellent ministry, inasmuch as He is also Mediator of a **better** covenant, which was established on **better** promises.*

One would think that this truth would be met with little resistance, but we have encountered nearly irrational thinking and behavior upon discussing it as if to simply state that we are not under the Old is to threaten the very existence of God Himself!

Let us be clear, we are absolutely not saying (as some have slanderously reported) that we should rip the Bible in half and throw away the Old Testament writings. On the contrary, we need Genesis – Malachi in order to fully appreciate the New Covenant, but that we are not under the Old Covenant is indisputable! In fact, if you are not Jewish by birth, at no time have you **ever** been under the Old Covenant for the Old Covenant was with the Jews **only**. As we have discussed, the law was meant to bring the Jewish people to Christ—serving as a tutor. But after faith has come, they (and we) are no longer under the tutelage of law (Gal. 3:25).

It is important that we understand not only that the two covenants are different, but that we see with acute clarity that the Old Covenant is now obsolete.

Hebrews 8:12-13
*For I will be merciful to their unrighteousness, and their sins and their lawless deeds I will remember no more." [13] In that He says, "A new covenant," **He has made the first obsolete.** Now what is becoming obsolete and growing old is ready to vanish away.*

When I worked as a teacher, each year the librarian would get out her rubber stamp and spend several hours stamping hundreds of textbooks and library books with the word "OBSOLETE". This meant that these books were no longer to be used in the school. Either the information in them had been found not to be true or the teaching methodology was considered not to be effective. The obsolete books were discarded and **replaced** with new books because the new books were considered *better*. (However, a few teachers, seeing that their favorite textbooks from which they taught for perhaps 10-20 years were going to be trashed, would somehow manage to keep a set of the obsolete books to use in the classroom.)

The Old Covenant was not capable of making us perfect or of allowing us to have perfect closeness with God. It could only make very clear to us that we were not perfect. The better hope that Jesus brought us not only perfects us forever in regard to sin and makes us holy (Heb. 10:9-14); but also brings us close to God. Under the Old Covenant, the presence of God was terrifying, and only the high priest dared enter. If his sacrifice was not accepted, he would die. This is not so for those who receive the New Covenant. His blood puts us permanently *in* the presence of God and puts His presence permanently in us! We live seated with Christ on the right hand of the throne of God.

Hebrews 4:14-16

Seeing then that we have a great High Priest who has passed through the heavens, Jesus the Son of God, let us hold fast our confession. [15] For we do not have a High Priest who cannot sympathize with our weaknesses, but was in all points tempted as we are, yet without sin. [16] Let us therefore come boldly to the throne of grace that we may obtain mercy and find grace to help in time of need.

When Jesus said that the law would not fall away until all was fulfilled (Matt. 5:18), many take this to mean that we are still under that law. Jesus was not saying any such thing. He was foretelling of the time when He Himself would fulfill the law for us. The Old Covenant had a purpose, and that purpose was fulfilled in Jesus Christ at His death.

Luke 24: 44-45
*Then He said to them, "These are the words which I spoke to you while I was still with you, that **all things must be fulfilled which were written in the Law of Moses and the Prophets and the Psalms concerning Me**." ⁴⁵ And He opened their understanding, that they might comprehend the Scriptures.*

Romans 8:3-4
*For what the law **could not do** in that it was weak through the flesh, God did by sending His own Son in the likeness of sinful flesh, on account of sin: He condemned sin in the flesh, ⁴ **that the righteous requirement of the law might be fulfilled in us** who do not walk according to the flesh but according to the Spirit.*

Did you hear that? The righteous requirement of the law has been fulfilled in us believers. God opens our eyes to understand the Old Covenant writers, but not in the sense of being tutored by them, but rather to see how Jesus perfectly fulfilled them. Once He fulfilled them, He replaced them. Now, He speaks to us through His Son.

Hebrews 1:1-3
*God, who at various times and in various ways spoke in time **past** to the fathers by the prophets, ² has in these last days spoken to us by His **Son**, whom He has appointed heir of all things, through whom also He made the worlds; ³ who being the brightness of His glory and the express image of His person, and upholding all things by the word of His power, when He had by Himself **purged** our sins, sat down at the right hand of the Majesty on high.*

The law was given to the Children of Israel for a season. The New Covenant was not God's Plan B because Plan A failed. It was always God's design that the law that came through Moses would be replaced by Jesus.

John 1:14-17

*And the Word became flesh and dwelt among us, and we beheld His glory, the glory as of the only begotten of the Father, full of grace and truth. [15] John bore witness of Him and cried out, saying, "This was He of whom I said, 'He who comes after me is preferred before me, for He was before me.'" [16] And of His fullness we have all received, and grace for grace. [17] For the **law** was given through Moses, but **grace and truth** came through Jesus Christ.*

Knowing that Jesus fulfilled the law we can rejoice that we are not under it. We can read all of Scripture from our New Covenant perspective—in its proper context.

When we read the blessings and curses of the law; instead of fearing the curses or thinking we must follow the law in order to receive its blessing, we can be thankful that we are already blessed in Him apart from following the law (2 Pet. 1:3; Eph. 1:3) and that the curses for disobeying the law have been broken (Gal. 3:13).

When we hear the longing of the Psalmist to be given a clean heart, we can overflow with gratitude that we already have one (2 Pet. 1:9). When David asks that God's Holy Spirit not be taken from him, we can sing out our praises that the Spirit abides in us forever (Jn. 14:16). When he expresses his concern that he not be cast away from God's presence, we can rejoice that this will never happen to those who are in Christ (Heb. 13:5). **In other words, we have those things for which those under the Old Covenant could only long.** Once we know who we are in Him and what He has already provided for us through the New Covenant, the Scriptures prior to His cross take on a more blessed significance and cause us to give thanks.

Jesus used the Scriptures concerning Himself with those he met on the road to Emmaus. The Early church as well taught Christ using Genesis through Malachi. They proved through the prophecies that Jesus was indeed the Christ. They gave evidence of what He would accomplish.

Acts 17:2
As usual, Paul went to the synagogue, and on three Sabbath days reasoned with them from the Scriptures.

Acts 17:11
The people here were more open-minded than those in Thessalonica, since they welcomed the message with eagerness and examined the Scriptures daily to see if these things were so.

Acts 18:24, 28
A Jew named Apollos, a native Alexandrian, an eloquent man who was powerful in the use of the Scriptures, arrived in Ephesus...[28] For he vigorously refuted the Jews in public, demonstrating through the Scriptures that Jesus is the Messiah.

What about the teachings of Christ? Some have said that nothing He taught speaks to believers at all because He spoke prior to the establishment of the New Covenant. This is not true. Yet, as I have already stated, in order to understand their true meaning, we must keep in mind that even the words of Jesus need to be considered in their context.

Allow me to reiterate a little here. When we read the words of Jesus, we need to discern if He was preparing His audience for what was to come, speaking a universal truth or if He was speaking to those who would be under the New Covenant. We do this by observing the context and the obvious intent of His words, but always interpreting them in light of the New Covenant *which was yet to come.*

Here is another splendid example.

Matthew 5:20
For I say to you, that unless your righteousness exceeds the righteousness of the scribes and Pharisees, you will by no means enter the kingdom of heaven.

If we do not understand the context of this saying, we will become discouraged. Jesus was speaking to the Jews. They knew the Scribes and Pharisees to be righteous according to the law (Phil. 3:6, Lk. 1:6). Jesus surprises them by saying that in order to enter the kingdom of God, their righteousness had to *exceed* that of the Scribes and Pharisees. This doubtless caused them to tremble. How could they ever be more righteous than those who were endeavoring so diligently to keep the law? Yet, Jesus knew something that those on that side of the cross did not yet know—that the righteousness that would exceed that of the Pharisees would be given as a *gift* to those who put their trust in Jesus. Only an imputed righteousness, the very righteousness of God, which we obtained as a gift when He became a sin offering for us, would be sufficient (2 Cor. 5:21). **Our righteousness thus *exceeds* the righteousness of the Scribes and Pharisees.**

No clearer proof can be given that we are under the New Covenant only and that our focus is now on Jesus, not the law and prophets, than what happened on the Mount of Transfiguration (Lk. 9:28-36). You know the story. Jesus took Peter, James, and John apart to a high mountain separately and was transfigured before them. While this was happening, Moses and Elijah appeared and spoke with Jesus about His upcoming death.[35] While Moses and Elijah were departing; Peter, not knowing what to say out of fear, proposed a tabernacle be built for each of them; one for Jesus, one for Moses, and one for Elijah, but God had something different in mind. He spoke from heaven and said, "This is my beloved SON. Hear HIM!" Previously, God spoke through the law and prophets, but now He is speaking to us through His Son Jesus (Heb. 1:1-2).

When we understand the dividing line between the Old and New Covenant to be the cross, we begin to appreciate the changes God brought about through the death, burial, and resurrection of His Son. Glory to God! We are under

---

[35] Moses represents the Law. Elijah represents the prophets.

the New Covenant *only*.[36] The Old Covenant is OBSOLETE. The life that we now live is through **faith** in the Son of God who loved us and gave Himself for us.

---

[36] The best chart I have encountered delineating the contrast between the Old Covenant and the New can be found in an article by James A. Fowler entitled "God's Covenants with Man", Number III. To view this chart, go to: http://www.christinyou.net/pages/covenants.html. Additionally, the book <u>Jesus Changes Everything</u> by Bob George goes into greater detail about the two covenants.

Day 12

REDEFINITION OF TERMS

---

*W*hen we became aware that we missed "the" gospel, we began a gradual process we called "the chopping block" reasoning that if we had not understood something as basic as the Christian life being a life of faith in response to His grace and not all about what we do and don't do to improve ourselves, then surely there were other areas in which we had erred. Everything we'd been taught about how to live the Christian life became subject to examination. Every supposed "spiritual" experience we'd known was evaluated. Our callings and gifts were also part of this assessment. As this process took place over several years we began to see a pattern developing and were able to gradually identify just *how* it was that we got off track.

One factor stands out to us as our most crucial error. Just as happens in a cult, terms were redefined. Once this happened a veil of misinterpretation was hung before us that kept us from seeing the truth. It was as if we had put on a pair of truth-dimming glasses that obscured the light, not allowing us to see what was actually written. Therefore we missed the truth in verses such as this.

Romans 16:25
*Now to Him who is able to **establish you** according to my **gospel** and the **preaching of Jesus Christ**,*

114

according to the revelation of the mystery kept secret since the world began.

First of all, as I've discussed, "the gospel", in our thinking, was what you preached to the lost. We never once considered that the gospel should be preached to the saved. Thus, each time we read the word "gospel" we assumed the text applied to non-believers and were blind as to how the passage might be directed at us, the saved. So in the above passage we didn't see that **the gospel *establishes* believers**.

Another blind spot we developed was that we saw "grace" only as what one needed to get saved, the ability to endure difficulties, or a kindness afforded to those who offend. Certainly, grace is all of these things, but grace is also **the gospel.**

Galatians 6:1
*I marvel that you are turning away so soon from Him who called you in **the grace of Christ**, to a **different** gospel.*

While we might at first be uncertain as to what Paul means by a "different" gospel, there can be no doubt from this passage that in his thinking the real gospel is "the grace of Christ".

In fact, Paul defined his entire ministry as the gospel of God's grace.

Acts 20:24
*But none of these things move me; nor do I count my life dear to myself, so that I may finish my race with joy, and **the ministry** which I received from the Lord Jesus, to testify to the **gospel of the grace of God**.*

As our studies continued we saw again and again that Paul, John, and Peter all saw God's **grace** as **the** gospel, not just an **aspect** of the gospel. To Titus, Paul said that **grace** *brings* salvation.

> **Titus 2:11**
> *For the **grace of God** has appeared, **bringing sal-vation** to all men.*

He wrote that the **gospel** which the Colossians heard and understood was the **grace of God**. This very grace was continually bearing fruit and increasing.

> **Colossians 1:5-6**
> *Because of the hope laid up for you in heaven, of which you previously heard in the word of truth, **the gospel** [6] which has come to you, just as in all the world also it is constantly bearing fruit and increasing, even as it has been doing in you also since the day you heard of it and understood **the grace of God** in truth.*

To the Corinthians he spoke of **the grace of God** which was **spreading**, and to the Ephesians he states that it is by **grace** that we are saved through faith.

> **2 Corinthians 4:15**
> *For all things are for your sakes, so that **the grace which is spreading to more and more people** may cause the giving of thanks to abound to the glory of God.*
> **Ephesians 2:8-9**
> *For **by grace** you have been saved through faith; and that not of yourselves, it is the **gift of God**; [9] not as a result of works, so that no one may boast.*

John wrote that grace and truth **came** through Jesus. Peter spoke of the prophets who foresaw our **salvation** as the **grace** that would come to us.

John 1:14, 16-17
*And the Word became flesh and dwelt among us, and we beheld His glory, the glory as of the only begotten of the Father, full of **grace** and truth... ^16 And of His fullness we have all received, and **grace for grace**. ^17 For the law was given through Moses, but **grace and truth came through Jesus Christ**.*

1 Peter 1:10
*As to this **salvation**, the prophets who prophesied of **the grace that would come to you** made careful searches and inquiries.*

Grace is the "glad tidings of good things" from our benevolent Father. It isn't just how we get saved—it's not the elementary principles that we leave behind after we understand them. It is the full counsel of God.[37] Grace is everything that God did and does for us. It is His undeserved and unmerited favor not only for the sinner, but toward us, His beloved children. It is undeserved because we have done plenty to disqualify ourselves from receiving it and unmerited because we can do nothing to earn it. He not only gave up His Son for us when we were His enemies; He now freely gives us all things! This is good news—for *believers*—the gospel of God's grace!

Romans 8:31-32
*What then shall we say to these things? If God is **for** us, who can be against us? ^32 He who did not spare His own Son, but delivered Him up for us all, how shall He not with Him **also** freely give (shall be graciously granting)[38] us all things?*

---

[37] Notice the context of the term "full counsel of God" is immediately following Acts 20:24 where Paul refers to his ministry as the gospel of God's grace. To him the gospel was the full counsel of God.

[38] Parenthesis from Greek Interlinear (http://www.scripture4all.org/OnlineInterlinear/NTpdf/rom8.pdf)

By redefining "gospel" and "grace", we missed the significance of multiple passages—nearly the entire impact of the gospel. Even Paul's greetings of grace were skipped over as mere salutations. As we began to embrace the fuller significance of these terms and others our understanding of Scripture came alive again, and we were able to return to the blessed enjoyment of our relationship with God.

Day 13

OUR MOST SACRED COW

*H*owever difficult redefining "the gospel" and "grace" made it for us to discern the importance of God's grace and to understand the need for the gospel to be preached to the saved, the most devastating redefinition of terms we embraced was our understanding of what Paul meant in his letters when he referred to "law". This confusion is still commonplace among believers today, contributes to promoting "another" gospel, and is robbing us of receiving and enjoying what Jesus accomplished by His sacrifice for us.

Theologians divide Old Covenant law into three basic categories: the ceremonial laws, the civil laws, and the moral laws also known as the Ten Commandments. After making these distinctions we conclude that when Paul spoke about the law, he was *only* referring to the ceremonial and civil laws and not the Ten Commandments.

Once we believed this premise, David and I became incapable of perceiving what Paul actually meant when he spoke of the law. Because of this blind spot we'd created by redefining "law", we never worried about nullifying the grace of God by moral law, nor were we concerned that living by moral law was implying that Christ's death was in vain. (Gal. 2:21). We saw "law" and immediately thought of Jewish ritual. When we read that no flesh would be justified before God by the deeds of the law (Rom. 3:20), we simply agreed that it was foolishness to think that by keeping the *ceremonial* law someone could be righteous before God.

These three divisions, while logical, are not inherent in the law but rather a conclusion to which *we* have come. In actuality, the law of Moses was *all* of the law given to Moses. Thus, when Paul wrote "law" in reference to the Old Covenant, *he* meant the entire law.

If we do not understand this, we miss the major components of why the New Covenant is "better". We end up setting aside the grace of God by mixing it with law, and the greatest accomplishments of His sacrifice are swept under the rug because we can't see them.

No topic has been met with more vitriol than this one, for the moral law is our most sacred cow. Ideas that we have believed, practiced, taught and defended tooth and nail for most our lives become something untouchable for us, and this is strikingly true with the commandments.

We *revere* the Ten Commandments. In the United States we legislate for the right to display them at our courthouses. We post them on our monuments and church walls. We go to great lengths to prove that each and every one of the commandments is mentioned within the New Testament writings. We develop lengthy teaching series about them and compose musicals to commemorate their importance and produce movies to prove how important they still are. We make sure our children memorize them. We follow them with all our might.

David and I were able to remain ignorant of the original, contemporary, and personal import of many of Paul's writings, especially Galatians and Romans, because when we read the word "law" we automatically *redefined* it in our thinking to mean *only* the ceremonial and civil laws of the Jews and not the moral law. We wouldn't have even *considered* touching the sacred Ten!

We, the church, have a difficult time rationally discussing this topic because the Ten Commandments are ingrained in our thinking and deeply set in our traditions. There is often a near automatic visceral response to any possibility that we don't need them as believers. We tend to ignore those who bid us to consider a differing theological point of view which would remove them from Christian living, so much so that I am guessing that many who are reading this chapter are right now getting ready to toss this book in the trash! When the conversation begins, if it begins, we pull a veil across our faces and ignore what is being said. We start labeling those who are trying to point out these truths so as to silence them. We put up our defenses and can't have an honest discussion because we are too emotionally involved. We roll our eyes far back into our head thinking that those who share such things are ignorant buffoons while we ourselves are hiding behind the veil we've closed, willfully ignoring clear Biblical evidence. We quote only the verses which *seem* to say that we are still under them, completely disregarding the scriptures that clearly say we are not.

We understand this reaction. At one, time the idea that anyone would believe that the Ten Commandments are no longer our ethical guide offended us to our core. Even after many years of understanding that we are not under "law", but grace, I still couldn't let go of them. Yet, when I finally understood that when Paul wrote "law", he meant *all* religious laws, everything else came into sharper focus and I began to see in Scripture what I could not see previously due to the veil I had closed.

Please allow me to explain why I believe that the Ten Commandments are not for Christians. If what I write here is inaccurate, you will be harmed in no way by reading it. If what I am saying is true, you will be set free. It really is so simple and obvious, that no lengthy explanation is even necessary. Father, open our eyes that your church might see!

In Exodus, we read that God miraculously delivered the Children of Israel out of captivity from Egypt where they worked as slaves. God opened the Red Sea and brought the them to Mt. Sinai. There God called Moses up to the mountain and God Himself wrote on **stone tablets** the Ten Commandments. Later, when Moses saw that the they had constructed a golden calf and were worshipping it while Moses was meeting with God, he threw the tablets to the ground and they were broken. However, God in His compassion called Moses back up into Mt. Sinai and the commandments of the Old Covenant were written again on stone tablets. Please pay close attention to these passages.

> ### Exodus 34:1, 27-28
> *And the LORD said to Moses, "Cut two tablets of stone like the first ones, and I will write on these **tablets** the words that were on the first tablets which you broke." Then the LORD said to Moses, "Write these words, for **according to the tenor of these words I have made a covenant with you and with Israel**." [28] So he was there with the LORD forty days and forty nights; he neither ate bread nor drank water. And He wrote on the **tablets the words of the covenant, the Ten Commandments**.*
>
> ### Deuteronomy 4:13
> *So He declared to you His **covenant** which He commanded you to perform, **the Ten Commandments;** and He wrote them on two **tablets of stone.***

How clearly obvious this is! The Old Covenant was the Ten Commandments. The Ten Commandments were His covenant. A person needs to do some mighty convoluted explaining to say otherwise. God Himself calls the Ten Commandments the "covenant" which He was making with Israel.

What is the status of this covenant? It is obsolete (Heb. 8:13). It is annulled.

> ### Hebrews 7:18-19
> *For on the one hand there is an **annulling** of the former **commandment** because of its weakness and unprofitableness, [19] for the **law** made nothing perfect; on the other hand, there is the bringing in of a **better hope**, through which we draw near to God.*

Understanding that the Ten Commandments *were* the Old Covenant and that the Old Covenant is obsolete and has been replaced with the better New Covenant, empowers us to more fully understand not only the writings of Paul but also guide us to comprehend what it means to live under grace and not under law.

What we should ask ourselves next is if there is any evidence within the *New* Testament writings that when Paul said "law" he was including the Ten Commandments? The answer is, yes!

Immediately after Paul stated that we are dead to the law (Rom. 7:1-6), it is made clear that he was including the Ten Commandments by quoting one of them.

Romans 7:7-11

What shall we say then? Is **the law** *sin? Certainly not! On the contrary, I would not have known sin except through* **the law.** *For I would not have known covetousness unless the* **law** *had said,* "**You shall not covet.**" [8] *But sin, taking opportunity by the* **commandment,** *produced in me all manner of evil desire. For apart from the* **law** *sin was dead.* [9] *I was alive once without the* **law,**[39] *but when the* **commandment** *came, sin revived and I died.*[40] [10] *And*

---

[39] Paul was born under the law and circumcised the eighth day. At no time was he "alive once without the law" until he was born again, for prior to that he was spiritually dead and under the law.

[40] Paul was freed from sin, but when the commandment came, sin was revived. We believe he is speaking about a personal experience when, being a Pharisee, he started to believe that even though he was saved by grace through faith, he also needed to obey the law. When this happened sin revived in him making it difficult to do what he knew was right and to stop doing what was wrong. **In other words, the law introduced into the believer's life, brings death.** Others deduce from this passage that Paul is referring to the unsaved man trying to live under law. Whatever conclusion one may assume, it is clear that Paul is blaming the law, including the Ten Commandments, for bringing death. The New American Bible Commentary for Romans 7:13-25 reads: **"Far from improving the sinner, law encourages**

*the **commandment**, which was to bring life, I found to bring death.[11] For sin, taking occasion by the **commandment**, deceived me, and by it killed me.*

It is significant that Paul quotes the tenth commandment, "You shall not covet," as what the *law* says and then goes on to refer to the *commandment*. When Paul wrote "law", he clearly intended to include the Ten Commandments, the very Ten Commandments to which he undoubtedly proclaims in this same context that we have died (Rom. 7:4).

He also makes some strong commentary on the law with clear evidence to the fact that he was including the entire law, specifically the Ten Commandments, stating that the "letter kills", referring to law as "the ministry of death", and reiterating that the commandments are "the ministry of condemnation".

2 Corinthians 3:4-11

*And we have such trust through Christ toward God. [5] Not that we are sufficient of ourselves to think of anything as being from ourselves, but our sufficiency is from God, [6] who also made us sufficient as ministers of the **new covenant**, **not of the letter** (not of the law) but of the Spirit; **for the letter kills**, but the Spirit gives life. [7] But if the **ministry of death**, **written and engraved on stones**, was glorious, so that the children of Israel could not look steadily at the face of Moses because of the glory of his countenance,*

---

sin to expose itself in transgressions or violations of specific commandments (see Romans 1:24; 5:20). Thus persons who do not experience the justifying grace of God, and *Christians* who revert to dependence on law as the criterion for their relationship with God, will recognize a rift between their reasoned desire for the goodness of the law and their actual performance that is contrary to the law. Unable to free themselves from the slavery of sin and the power of death, they can only be rescued from defeat in the conflict by the power of God's grace working through Jesus Christ."

which glory was passing away, [8] how will the ministry of the Spirit not be more glorious? [9] For if the **ministry of condemnation** *had glory, the ministry of righteousness exceeds much more in glory. [10] For even what was made glorious had no glory in this respect, because of the glory that excels. [11] For if what is passing away was glorious, what remains is much more glorious.*

The "letter", which is the ministry of death and condemnation, is clearly referring to the whole law and even more specifically to the Ten Commandments in this passage (and not to the written word, as some have falsely assumed). Which ministry do we live under: the ministry of death and condemnation which kills or the ministry of the Spirit and of righteousness which gives life?

If Paul were to preach like this in many of our churches today, he would be expelled immediately. Imagine saying that the Ten Commandments revive sin in our lives—that they kill and condemn. That would be to attack in no uncertain terms our most holy livestock!

Paul who makes the amazing claim that he was "blameless" in respect to the righteousness in the law in Philippians 3:6, declares in the same passage that He considered that law-based righteousness was "rubbish" which he forsook in order to obtain the righteousness that comes through faith alone. We don't mind him saying that he forsook self-righteousness or even his religious pedigree, but if he were to visit a church and clarify that he was referring to the righteousness gained by keeping the entire law including the sacred Ten as "garbage", would any pastor invite him back?

As long as we insist that the moral laws are excluded from Paul's teachings about the law, we cannot understand what he is saying about how we now live. In fact, his teachings lose their significance almost entirely.

However painful it might be for us to recognize these truths, how can we go on feeding a sacred cow to which we are now dead; one which brings death and condemnation and empowers sinful passions in our lives? How can we continue purporting something as necessary when God declares that we are dead to it and that it has been annulled and is now obsolete?

The only way to continue in this false teaching is to cover our eyes, plug our ears and begin singing, "Tradition! Tradition!" Go ahead; sing it louder and louder until you can no longer hear this glorious truth that we are **dead** to the Ten Commandments.

Not until we hear what Paul was truly saying when he spoke of the law will we be able to fathom the depths of the Holy Spirit's message to us through his letters. When we reread them with the understanding that when he writes "law", he means the *entire* law, only then can we begin to understand the glorious accomplishments of the cross.

Beloved, we are free from the entire Old Covenant. We are under the New Covenant only. Mixing law back into grace by excluding the Ten Commandments from what Paul meant when He wrote "law", is to preach "another" gospel, for if righteousness can come from keeping any part of the law, then Christ died unnecessarily (Gal.2:21).

Day 14

PIVOTAL MOMENT OF TRUTH

*H*ow shocking it must have been for the Jews who always separated themselves from the Gentiles, seeing them as unclean, to witness that God was extending salvation to them as well! To some it might have been a wonderful marvel, but to others something repugnant and abhorrent. Yet, one of the most glorious truths of this New Covenant is that God made both Jew and Gentile one, based on faith in Jesus.

> **Ephesians 2:14-18**
> *For He Himself is our peace, who has made both one, and has broken down the middle wall of separation, 15 having abolished in His flesh the enmity, that is, the **law of commandments contained in ordinances,** so as to create in Himself one new man from the two, thus making peace, 16 and that He might reconcile them both to God in one body through the cross, thereby putting to death the enmity. 17 And He came and preached peace to you who were afar off and to those who were near. 18 For through Him we both have access by one Spirit to the Father.*

The shock of this union is easy for one to overlook if one lives in a culture which is predominantly already accepting of different races, cultures, and religions, but we need to take into account the wall that divided Jew and Gentile for so many centuries, so that we can begin to perceive that this brought about some major disputes. One of those crucial clashes pertains to the question of whether or not the Ten Commandments are essential for believers. Imagine the scene recorded in Acts 15, for example. Certain Jewish believers from Judea insisted that, "Unless you are circumcised according to the custom of Moses, you cannot be saved," referring to the Gentiles who were already believers. Of course, we wouldn't hesitate to repudiate such nonsense as we are convinced that circumcision is not required for continued salvation. This demand brought about "no small dissension" between them, and Paul and Barnabas. After no resolution to this dispute, the elders "determined that Paul and Barnabas and certain others of them should go up to Jerusalem, to the apostles and elders, about this question."

Along their way, as they passed through Phoenicia and Samaria, they told the Christians there about the conversion of the Gentiles. This "caused great joy to all the brethren." When they came to Jerusalem, Paul and Barnabas were received by the church, apostles, and elders, and they told them of what God had been doing among the Gentiles. Yet, not everyone was pleased.

Acts 15:5-11
*But some of the sect of the Pharisees who believed rose up, saying, "It is necessary to circumcise them, **and** to command them to keep the Law of Moses." 6 Now the apostles and elders came together to consider this matter. 7 And when there had been **much dispute**, Peter rose up and said to them: "Men and brethren, you know that a good while ago God chose among us, that by my mouth the Gentiles should hear the word of the gospel and believe. 8 So God, who knows the heart, acknowledged them by giving them the Holy Spirit, just as He did to us, 9 and made no distinction between us and them, purifying their*

hearts by faith. ¹⁰ *Now therefore, why do you test God by putting a yoke on the neck of the disciples which neither our fathers nor we were able to bear?* ¹¹ *But we believe that through the **grace** of the Lord Jesus Christ we **shall be** saved in the same manner as they."*[41]

In verse five we read that this was not only about circumcision, but as to whether or not the Gentiles needed to keep the law of Moses in its entirety. Just as Paul wrote, he who is circumcised must keep the whole law.

Galatians 5:3
*And I testify again to every man who becomes circumcised that he is a debtor to keep the **whole** law.*

"Much dispute" followed, much like it does today when this topic is discussed. If *we* hold the commandments in such high regard, imagine how much more the Jews did. It's the question at hand. Were believers then and are believers today required to keep the whole law?

The "yoke on the neck of the disciples which neither our father nor we were able to bear" was clearly the law of Moses. Peter stated that it is to "test God" to tell believers that they need to keep the law of Moses to be right with God. He made it abundantly clear, that our hearts "are purified by faith" and we are saved (initially, continually, and ultimately) by the **grace** of God.

At this point, the multitude that gathered to consider this issue kept silent as they heard of the many miracles God had worked among the Gentiles. Then James came to this conclusion in verses 19-20.

Therefore I judge that we should not trouble those from among the Gentiles who are turning to God, ²⁰ *but that we*

---

[41] Notice again grace as opposed to the law of Moses.

write to them to abstain from things polluted by idols, from sexual immorality, from things strangled, and from blood.

Then, a letter was written to the Gentile brothers to confirm the decision of the Jerusalem council (Acts 15:23-29).

The apostles, the elders, and the brethren,
*To the **brethren** who are of the Gentiles in Antioch, Syria, and Cilicia:*
Greetings.
*24 Since we have heard that some who went out from us have troubled you with words, unsettling your souls, saying, "You must be circumcised **and** keep the law" —to whom we gave no such commandment— 25 it seemed good to us, being assembled with one accord, to send chosen men to you with our beloved Barnabas and Paul, 26 men who have risked their lives for the name of our Lord Jesus Christ. 27 We have therefore sent Judas and Silas, who will also report the same things by word of mouth. 28 For it seemed good to the Holy Spirit, and to us, to lay upon you no greater burden than these necessary things: 29 that you abstain from things offered to idols, from blood, from things strangled, and from sexual immorality. If you keep yourselves from these, you will do well.*
Farewell.

Please consider the following question. **If keeping the Ten Commandments is required for believers, why didn't the council simply admonish the Gentiles to keep the Ten Commandments at this very crucial point in church history?** The first three instructions they gave would have been covered by the first commandment, and the fourth by the seventh.

The most logical answer to this query is that the elders understood the significance of the question at hand and the consequence of their response: Was something beyond faith in Christ necessary for the Gentile disciples (those who were already Christians) to be right with God? Going back to verse 8-10 we see that both Jew and Gentile are saved by the grace of God through faith in Christ, not by following the law of Moses. To have asked the Gentiles to keep the Ten Commandments would have been to say yes, keeping the law is *also* necessary for continued salvation.

Our salvation is by God's grace alone through faith in Christ alone. There is no law necessary to be saved nor is there a law needed for our continued or ultimate salvation. Even the "necessary things" they listed were not given as conditions for salvation but only that they would "do well" by abiding by them.

This truth cannot be minimized. **The New has not *merged* with the Old. It has *replaced* the Old.** New Covenant righteousness is based on **faith** in Jesus. Old Covenant righteousness was based on **keeping** the law— the entire law. Right-standing with God is based on believing instead of doing—can you see this?

Yet we, the church, have created a mixture of the two. This mixture is what Paul is warning the Galatians to forsake who were adding law to grace.

Many in the church today teach that we are saved by grace through faith, but that after that our relationship with God is maintained and improved by keeping laws; not only the Ten Commandments but many other traditions and "disciplines" which **we** have developed. This heresy of adding law to grace is as old as the Early Church, and I believe that we are far worse now than then because we've had two thousand years to add on and refine more and more and more expectations so that now it is almost impossible to even be born again without adding requirements beyond faith.

Take for example the idea that in order to be saved one must, as *we* say "make Jesus the Lord of your life". Paul had no such thought in his mind when he wrote Romans 10:9-13.

*If you confess with your mouth **the** Lord Jesus and believe in your heart that God has raised Him from* *the dead, you will be saved. ¹⁰ For with the heart one* **believes** *unto righteousness, and with the mouth* **confession** *is made unto salvation. ¹¹ For the Scripture says, "Whoever* **believes** *on Him will not be put to shame." ¹² For there is no distinction between Jew and Greek, for the same Lord over all is rich to all who call upon Him. ¹³* **For "whoever calls on the name of the Lord shall be saved.***"

Paul does not say that we need to confess Him as *our* Lord, but as *the* Lord. There is a big difference. The trouble with the former is that it would be to say that something in addition to faith is necessary for salvation and **this is clearly not the case** (Eph. 2:8-9). Yet before the sinner has his foot in the door we have burdened him down with the law of making Jesus the Lord of every aspect of his life. Paul is not asking the penitent heart to promise God that Jesus will be the Lord of His life from now on *in order* to be saved, but rather to believe that Jesus is *God.*

The name "Lord" is Kurios which in the Greek version of the Old Testament is used for the august name "Jehovah," and by its use, implies deity. Thus, to confess Jesus as Lord includes a heart belief in His deity, incarnation, vicarious atonement and bodily resurrection. Robertson says, "No Jew would do this who had not really trusted Christ, for Kurios in the LXX⁴² is used of God. No Gentile would do it who had not ceased worshipping the emperor as kurios. The word Kurios was and is the touchstone of faith."⁴³

Do we, the church, have so little faith in the grace of God that we feel we must do this preventative intervention

---

⁴² The LLX is the Septuagint version of the Old Testament which is the Hebrew Bible translated into Greek.

⁴³ Wuest's Word Studies–Wuest's Word Studies – Volume 1: Word Studies in the Greek New Testament.

before someone is even saved? Do we think if we can get them to the point of being at least willing to make Jesus their personal Lord, then after salvation, they will have this in mind and have a better chance of living right? Or even worse, do we actually *believe* that something beyond faith in Christ is necessary for salvation? God forbid!

Yes, it's true, at salvation Jesus is our Lord, but salvation isn't based on us *making* Him Lord, but on us *believing* He is *the* Lord. If this is not true, then none of us are yet saved. Have we made Jesus the Lord of *every* area of our lives yet—every thought, every word, every deed? How long have we been serving Him? If our answer is, "Well, I'm working on it," or "I mean that I'm *willing* for Him to be the Lord of every area of my life eventually," then we haven't made Him our Lord yet and we aren't saved yet; that is, if making Him the Lord of our lives is required for salvation.

When we read through the book of Acts, we don't see this concept of confessing Jesus as "our" Lord being mentioned even once. There is no recorded "sinner's prayer" either. People simply put their faith in Jesus Christ and they were gloriously saved and baptized. Surely today, such a salvation experience would be considered "easy believism".

The Philippian jailer asked Paul and Silas, "Sirs, what must I do to be saved?" They simply replied, "Believe on **the Lord** Jesus Christ, and you will be saved, you and your household," (Acts 16:29-30), and they were saved.

Even confessing the exact words, "Jesus is the Lord," was not a set formula. For example, after hearing Philip explain what he'd been reading, the Ethiopian eunuch asked, "Here's water. What hinders me from being baptized?" and Philip responded, "If you **believe** with all of your heart, you may." What does he then say? "I believe that Jesus is the Son of God," and then Philip baptized him without telling him he needed to make Jesus his Lord, without asking him to confess his sins, and without adding any admonishment to keep the law (Acts 8:36-38).

Ephesians 2:8-9

*For by grace you have been saved through faith, and that not of yourselves; it is the **gift** of God, ⁹ **not** of works, lest anyone should boast.*

Clearly, we are born again by heart belief in the resurrection of Jesus Christ and confession that He is *the* Lord, and not by making Him "the Lord of my life". He *is* the Lord, the Lord God! When we confess Him as *the* Lord, we are made new creations, and gradually, by His love's wooing, by His grace that teaches us, He becomes the Lord over our lives.

The Early Church set the precedent for whether or not believers are required to keep the moral law. The burden which they and their forefathers were not able to bear is not ours to carry either. We are free from law—all of it, so that we can serve in newness of life.

Day 15

DOES GOD CARE ABOUT OXEN AND WINESKINS?

*T*here are interesting nuggets of truth to be found when reading the law that even those under the law didn't fully understand. For example, Paul quotes the law to make a point about supporting those who are in ministry.

> **1 Corinthians 9:9-10**
> *For it is written in the law of Moses, "You shall not muzzle an ox while it treads out the grain." Is it oxen God is concerned about? ¹⁰ Or does He say it altogether for our sakes? For our sakes, no doubt, this is written, that he who plows should plow in hope, and he who threshes in hope should be partaker of his hope.*

Jesus also said many things that His disciples could not fully understand until after He had risen and they were born again. For example, consider what He said about sewing new cloth onto old and putting new wine into old wineskins.

> **Luke 5:36-39**
> *Then He spoke a parable to them: "No one puts a piece from a new garment on an old one; otherwise the new makes a tear, and also the piece that was*

taken out of the new does not match the old. ³⁷ And no one puts new wine into old wineskins; or else the new wine will burst the wineskins and be spilled, and the wineskins will be ruined. ³⁸ But new wine must be put into new wineskins, and both are preserved. ³⁹ And no one, having drunk old wine, immediately desires new; for he says, 'The old is better.'"

Once the old wineskin serves its purpose, its usefulness is done. New wine must be put into new wineskins. Similarly, trying to patch an old garment with a new cloth will not fix the old garment but will result in an even worse tear.

What is Jesus saying? Does God care about garment and wineskins? Is He saying this to spare us the trauma of our clothing being torn or our wineskins bursting? Or does He say it for our sakes?

Here's what I believe Jesus was saying, that would later be revealed to the disciples. We can't patch what was lacking in the Old Covenant with the New Covenant, and you can't contain the New Covenant in the Old. It won't work. The Old Covenant was annulled by the New. The Old Covenant is now obsolete. It could never contain the New. We can only live in the New.

Take a closer look at Luke 5:39 above. Recently, as I was formatting my husband's teaching notes, I "saw" this verse for the "first" time. I said right out loud, "I don't ever remember reading that verse before." When I asked David about it, he said, "I know! Isn't that stunning?"

"And no one, having drunk old wine, immediately desires new; for he says, 'The old is better.'"

Is the Old "better" than the New or as the NASB puts it "good enough"? I'm confident that we could get everyone to agree that no, it isn't. Yet, this verse speaks of the tendency we have to feel more comfortable with the way things have always been done and the things we've always believed even if our wine skins are bursting.

All of us are persuaded from Scripture that the Old is not good enough. It isn't better. What Jesus accomplished on the cross is so far superior to the law of Moses, that it hardly seems fair to compare them. So if the Old isn't better than the New; if it isn't good enough, why do we insist on mixing the Old with the New at just about every opportunity? Why do we teach law, patching it with grace here and there? Why do we try to put God's glorious grace in the context of law? Any attempt will result in tragic loss and misery. God forbid that we would settle for something less than what Jesus provides.

$\mathcal{D}ay$ 16

ALL LAW

$\mathcal{L}$et us consider other examples of how the New Covenant has been poured into the Old. I'm not exclusively speaking now of the moral law, but the very law *system* itself. For example, under the law, blessings were promised to those who kept the law—completely.

Deuteronomy 28:1-2
*"Now it shall come to pass, if you diligently obey the voice of the Lord your God, to observe carefully **all** His commandments which I command you today, that the Lord your God will set you high above all nations of the earth. ² And all these blessings shall come upon you and overtake you, because you obey the voice of the Lord your God.*

Under the New Covenant we are blessed because of what Jesus accomplished on the cross and not because we keep commandments.

Ephesians 1:3
*Blessed be the God and Father of our Lord Jesus Christ, who **has** blessed us with **every** spiritual blessing in the heavenly places in Christ.*

2 Peter 1:1-4
To those who have obtained like precious faith with us by the righteousness of our God and Savior Jesus Christ:
*² Grace and peace be multiplied to you in the knowledge of God and of Jesus our Lord, ³ as His divine power **has given** to us **all** things that pertain to life **and** godliness, through the knowledge of Him who called us by glory and virtue.*

The Old Covenant pronounced curses upon those who did not diligently keep ALL of the law.

Deuteronomy 28:15
*"But it shall come to pass, if you do not obey the voice of the Lord your God, to observe carefully **all** His commandments and His statutes which I command you today, that all these curses will come upon you and overtake you.*

But praise God, with the New we are free from the curse of the law, and our sins and lawless deeds are remembered no more.

Galatians 3:13-14
*Christ has **redeemed** us from the curse of the law, having become a curse **for** us (for it is written, "Cursed is everyone who hangs on a tree"), ¹⁴ that the **blessing** of Abraham might come upon the Gentiles in Christ Jesus, that we might receive the promise of the Spirit through faith.*
Jeremiah 31:34
*"For I will forgive their iniquity, and their sin I will remember **no more**."*
Romans 4:8
*Blessed is the man to whom the LORD shall **not** impute sin.*

This system of being blessed for doing what is right and cursed for not doing what is commanded is an obvious message of many Sunday sermons. For example, how many times have we heard these blessings and curses quoted to motivate believers to give?

Malachi 3:8-10
"Will a man rob God?
Yet you have robbed Me!
But you say,
'In what way have we robbed You?'
In tithes and offerings.
*⁹ **You are cursed with a curse**,*
For you have robbed Me,
Even this whole nation.
¹⁰ Bring all the tithes into the storehouse,
That there may be food in My house,
And try Me now in this,"
Says the Lord of hosts,
"If I will not open for you the windows of heaven
And pour out for you such blessing
That there will not be room enough to receive it.

Are believers under this curse? Absolutely not! We are under no curse at all and most specifically when it relates to keeping the law of Moses. Jesus became a curse for us. Yet, it is being taught by some today that one of the reasons believers face difficulties such as poverty and sickness is because they aren't tithing and giving offerings. Imagine telling someone who has just lost his job that this wouldn't have happened if he had been giving ten percent, or telling a sick or homeless woman that in order to be healed or prosper, she must begin tithing! I'm not making this up. I have read this in books, heard it in sermons, and have listened to the pain of those who have been told that the reason their life is such a mess is because they are not tithing.

This is what the law system does: it causes us to link every event in our lives to whether or not we have been following it well enough.

Paul had something very different to say to the Galatians who were being taught that they needed to add law to grace.

Galatians 3:5
Therefore He who supplies the Spirit to you and works miracles among you, does He do it by the works of the law, or by the hearing of faith?—

Beloved, we actually taught and were instructed that in order for miracles to break out, we had to live holy lives, fast, pray, attend church, give, and on and on and on! Yet, what does Paul ask the Galatians and what is the rhetorical response? No! The Holy Spirit is ours by faith. The working of miracles is by faith. They do not come by keeping law or our religious effort or our personal holiness.

Acts 3:11-12
*Now as the lame man who was healed held on to Peter and John, all the people ran together to them in the porch which is called Solomon's, greatly amazed. 12 So when Peter saw it, he responded to the people: "Men of Israel, why do you marvel at this? **Or why look so intently at us, as though by our own power or godliness we had made this man walk?***

If we can understand this, the miracles for which we are so diligently working to see, will simply happen. Peter made it very clear. It's not because of our personal godliness. It's not because of our own power or effort. It is by grace through faith! **We can't *earn* miracles.**

Acts 3:16
And His name, through faith in His name, has made this man strong, whom you see and know. Yes, the faith which comes through Him has given him this perfect soundness in the presence of you all.

Some of us will readily agree that miracles can't be gained through our own godliness or power. Most concur that as believers in Jesus Christ we are not under any curse. Yet many Christians today cling to the other side of the equation of the law—that we are blessed *if* we do what is right. We tend to believe that God will "open the windows of heaven and pour out a blessing" we cannot contain *if* we will tithe and give offerings—if we will pray and read the Bible—if we will fast—if we will live uprightly—if we, if we, if we.

Friends, allow me to declare with exceeding great joy that the windows of heaven are already open to us under the New Covenant and His blessings are poured out upon us even "if we" don't deserve them! That's what grace is—**undeserved** favor from God. He has placed us in His kingdom. He has made us His righteousness. These blessings of the kingdom are based on what *Jesus* did, not as a result of what *we* do. They are based on His power working within us.

Ephesians 3:20
*Now to Him who is able to do exceedingly abundantly above all that we ask or think, **according to the power that works in us**, ²¹ to **Him** be glory in the church by Christ Jesus to all generations, forever and ever. Amen.*

Under the New Covenant, who can boast? Only Jesus receives the glory for the blessings we enjoy. We no longer live under the law system of being blessed for obeying law and cursed for not obeying law. Jesus became a curse for us to redeem us from the curse of the law. We now live under the New Covenant of grace which causes us to *receive* what *He* has done *for* us *apart* from keeping the law.

Galatians 3:11-14
But that no one is justified by the law in the sight of
God is evident, for "the just shall live by faith." ¹² Yet
the law is not of faith, but "the man who does them
shall live by them." ¹³ Christ has redeemed us from
the curse of the law, having become a curse for us
(for it is written, "Cursed is everyone who hangs on
a tree"), ¹⁴ that the blessing of Abraham might come
upon the Gentiles in Christ Jesus, that we might
receive the promise of the Spirit through faith.

Now before some of you begin to draw that curtain I
mentioned earlier, please consider my points. Why do we go
on insisting that New Covenant believers are under *certain*
parts of the law? Yes, the *Jews* were definitely cursed for
not tithing. Tithes and offerings were *required* under the Old
Covenant law. They *had* robbed God. They *were* cursed
with a curse because they were not obeying the law; but
beloved, we are under no such curse because we are not
under the law, not any part of it.

Even if we continue insisting that we are still under the
moral law, certainly we must acknowledge that tithing was
part of the *ceremonial* law which most agree we aren't under.

Yes, it's true, Jesus did tell the *Jewish* audience *who*
were under the law that they "did well" to tithe their mint and
rue. Are Christians required to tithe mint and rue? If we are
then I surely hope all of you who garden are putting aside
ten percent of what you produce—exactly ten percent, and
giving it to your pastor. Count those fruit and vegetables
and make sure you don't go under ten percent or you will be
cursed—that is if you believe you are blessed and cursed
for tithing *everything.*

Dear God, help us to understand the importance of this.

Some argue that since tithing took place before the law,
the practice of tithing supersedes the law and thus sets an
example for us. They will point to the tithe that Abraham

143

gave to Melchizedek as their "proof". Yet Abraham tithed only one time to Melchizedek and not from his *personal* possessions but only from the spoils of war. Additionally, he did this not as a requirement or by divine instruction, but from his heart. The true lesson regarding Melchizedek in Hebrews is not that we should tithe today but rather about the need for another priesthood apart from the Levitical priesthood—One from the tribe of Judah!

It is important to also consider that in every instance of tithing before the law, the desire and determination to do so came from the heart of the giver and not as a request or requirement or even as a divine revelation from God. Furthermore, we cannot use "the law of first mention" to argue that because people tithed before the law it is something *we* should do unless we are going to also practice other things that were performed before the law such as animal sacrifice and circumcision. Let us be consistent. If we are to follow this logic all the way through, some of us will need to circumcise our sons and build a stone altar in the backyard for sacrifices.[44]

Why is the supposed requirement to tithe or the promise of a blessing for tithing *never* mentioned, not even once in Matthew through Revelation? If tithing is imperative, especially to the extent that many teach—that we are cursed for not tithing, why didn't God make this clearer to us?

Why don't we have at least one record of a request from Jesus that his followers give ten percent? There He was—the King of kings and Lord of lords. We don't even have a record of anyone giving Him a tithe while He walked the earth. Why didn't He say, "Blessed are those who tithe, for the windows of heaven shall open to them,"? The way I've heard this preached in the past, it would seem one of the most ungodly things ever not to give ten percent. Why

---

[44] Do you find this bizarre? Our friend from Nigeria tells us that her "Christian" church there does perform animal sacrifices! In fact, she was shunned for asking what this practice accomplished and spent many years thinking she had committed "the unpardonable sin" for doubting.

didn't the Jerusalem council tell the Gentiles to avoid meat offered to idols, fornication, and to be sure to tithe? Why didn't Paul teach tithing when he taught on giving? He could have made it succinctly clear when he spoke of the oxen treading the corn in 1 Corinthians 9. Or he might have pointed it out in 2 Corinthians 8-9, for example. He could have quoted Malachi just as he so often quoted other Old Testament Scripture to make a point. It's not mentioned by *any* of the New Testament writers. Of all the correction in the book of Revelation there is none about not tithing; not even about a lack of giving. What does Paul say instead?

2 Corinthians 9:7
*So let each one give as **he** purposes in **his** heart, not grudgingly **or of necessity**; for God loves a cheerful giver.*

We don't give because we have to, and we aren't to give against our wills. We give as *we* purpose in our hearts, not an amount determined by God,[45] because God loves a cheerful giver. Remember, God is looking at the heart, not the amount. He loves the cheerfulness with which we give.[46]

Jesus spoke of such a giving that doesn't keep an account.

Matthew 6:1-4
"Take heed that you do not do your charitable deeds before men, to be seen by them. Otherwise you have no reward from your Father in heaven.

---

[45] This is not to say that God never puts an amount on our hearts. He may well tell us to help someone or give a certain amount, but even so, this is from our willing and cheerful hearts.

[46] I've also heard it taught that under the New Covenant that we give **all** (not a *mere* ten percent) as it appears the Early Church did by selling lands and supplying the needs of those who lacked, but this cannot be substantiated, and the person teaching this isn't performing such a thing either but usually only seeking to make his audience "settle" for ten percent instead of "all" when neither one is required.

² Therefore, when you do a charitable deed, do not sound a trumpet before you as the hypocrites do in the synagogues and in the streets, that they may have glory from men. Assuredly, I say to you, they have their reward. ³ But when you do a charitable deed, do not let your left hand know what your right hand is doing, ⁴ that your charitable deed may be in secret; and your Father who sees in secret will Himself reward you openly."

I remember as a young believer wondering how this verse could be true if we had to make a calculation of ten percent before giving. Surely, my right hand would know what my left was doing. Can we imagine giving with such abandon that we don't even really know how much we gave?

Believers don't need to worry about blessings and curses, for we cannot be cursed and we are already blessed. We can give freely because we have the peace that God will supply all of our needs.

2 Corinthians 9:6-7
*But this I say: He who sows sparingly will also reap sparingly, and he who sows bountifully will also reap bountifully. ⁷ So let each one give as he purposes in his heart, not grudgingly or of necessity; for God loves a cheerful giver. ⁸ And **God is able to make all grace abound toward you, that you, always having all sufficiency in all things, may have an abundance for every good work.***
Philippians 4:10, 14-19
*But I rejoiced in the Lord greatly that now at last your care for me has flourished again; though you surely did care, but you lacked opportunity… ¹⁴ Nevertheless you have done well that you shared in my distress. ¹⁵ Now you Philippians know also that in the beginning of the gospel, when I departed from Macedonia, **no church shared with me concerning giving and receiving but you only**. ¹⁶ For even in Thessalonica*

you sent aid once and again for my necessities.
¹⁷ Not that I seek the gift, but I seek the fruit that
abounds to your account. ¹⁸ Indeed I have all and
abound. I am full, having received from Epaphroditus
the things I sent from you, a sweet-smelling aroma,
an acceptable sacrifice, well pleasing to God. ¹⁹ **And**
my God shall supply all your need according to
His riches in glory by Christ Jesus.

Let me say this another way. Just as I have shown that
not being under the law but under grace gives us freedom
from sin's dominion instead of giving us freedom to sin; so it
is that not being under the law of tithing but under grace sets
us free to give abundantly—often far beyond ten percent as
we see took place in the Early Church.

Now, tithing is only one example of how we add law to
grace. Allow me to share a few more so that you may begin
to see with increasing clarity what Paul was talking about
when he warned not to receive "another" gospel.

Paul not only spoke of the law of Moses, but of law in
general. I'm not referring to the laws of our society for Paul
teaches us to obey these authorities in Romans 13. Paul is
discussing any law that is added to faith, religious laws, "for if
righteousness comes through law, then Christ died in vain."

The time has come to recognize that most of our
teachings are usually laced with law and that most of
the misery Christians experience in life is due to some
law that is lurking in their minds.

No one had to tell me to pray when I returned to faith
in Jesus as a young adult. I was praying "without ceasing".
Reading the word of God was an adventure and joy. I
rejoiced in learning that the God who made everything
loved me. The first thing I wanted to do after confessing
Jesus was find fellowship. Before a week had ended, I was
in church, and attending with my fellow believers became
my favorite pastime. Getting involved in ministry was all I
wanted from life. Loving God and pleasing God was my
constant aim. Rising up within me was this keen desire to

love my brothers and sisters. Giving was a joy! Sin was

love my brothers and sisters. Giving was a joy! Sin was falling from my life, right and left. Evil thoughts and desires were disappearing as I recognized daily how deeply I was loved. Every part of my life was being changed, even the words that came out of my mouth, the thoughts that came to my mind, and the types of activities in which I participated. Anyone who was brave enough to speak to me in those days got to hear of the glorious things God was doing in my life. I couldn't help but share His amazing grace. I remember thinking that the worthless things that I valued in my life before Christ were nothing compared to what He was giving to me, and I hadn't given them up in order to receive from God, but I gave them up because His love was daily overwhelming me.

None of these things happened as a result of any sermon I heard. God's grace was teaching me to "deny ungodliness and worldly lusts", to "live soberly, righteously, and godly in the present age", and to "love one another as I have loved you". His grace. His amazing grace! Not law.

As ministers, we observe the enthusiasm of new believers and perhaps wonder how it is that this passion so often dwindles over time. **I've come to see that we, the church, are teaching it out of them by adding laws and disciplines to grace which eventually results in setting grace aside.**

God wants us to be motivated by grace and led by His Spirit, not threatened by law and provoked by shame. Do you work well under this type of pressure? Take marriage or friendship for example. Is your idea of a happy relationship one in which you are bullied into compliance, punished for disobedience, or rewarded with for good behavior? God forbid! The new creation God made us was never meant to be under law. **We can't be completely at peace and free when "living" under the law system or if we *combine* law with grace.** It isn't what God intended when He gave His only Son.

Perhaps it's because we don't entirely trust God's grace in the lives of others. Instead of leaving people alone to pray to their heart's content without a structure every minute of every day, we have to impose a man-made standard of a certain amount of minutes each day devoted *only* to prayer. That way, we and they can keep an account. We rob people of the joy of constant relationship and replace it with religion at every opportunity by setting man-made goals of praying one hour or two or we devise systems so that constant prayer will be offered. On top of that some teach that if we don't read the Bible daily, we will eventually fall away and for this reason prescribe a certain amount of reading a day or a certain study program completely ignoring the fact that the first believers turned the world upside down without individually owning a Bible in the form we have it today. Witnessing becomes unnatural and stiff and intimidating as we teach program after program of how to present the gospel. Faith is replaced with fear at every corner. Service becomes mandatory instead of a ministry born out of love.

If we see a believer struggling, do we teach them of what Jesus has done to help them? Not usually. Customarily, we prescribe some sort of formula for them to fix themselves or their situation. If their children are acting up, we promote "tough love". If their marriage is failing, we give them the latest marriage book or send them to a marriage conference (usually one of the spouses dragging the other against his/ her will). If they are struggling with sin, do we teach them why they are free from sin? Not normally. It seems much easier to load more laws upon them.

Beloved, we are robbing God's sheep of the joy of their salvation by teaching formula living and behavior modification instead of teaching what Christ accomplished for us, and who He made us as a *gift*, and by not allowing the love and joy that comes from that knowledge to guide them.

We don't openly believe in "beating the sheep", but many do it almost weekly without even knowing it sometimes. The same formula is employed continuously. We whack them with, "This is what is wrong with you," then smack them saying, "And this is what *you* need to do to fix it." **We seldom proclaim what *Jesus* has done to help them.** Why, some sheep are so used to being beaten up on Sundays that if they don't feel the pastor "read their mail" by pointing out their faults, they don't feel as if they've "been to church". Think of this because it is entirely sick and dreadfully sad. They are like broken down children who are so accustomed to abuse that they are actually comforted by it.

Each and every week, 52 weeks a year, year after year for decades they hear how they are not measuring up. Is it any wonder that many sheep just give up? We are tempted to think they aren't coming to church because *they* lack commitment or are falling away, or perhaps we blame ourselves for not being dynamic enough, but could it be possible that some of them are smart enough to escape our abuse or that God, in His infinite mercy, is *leading* them away from us?

God's sheep are starving and emaciated and the church is largely to blame. Instead of feeding them the milk and meat of the word of God, we've fed them fodder. Most churches these days don't even teach basic doctrines such as the nature of God, the deity of Jesus Christ, and His second coming let alone the *"glad tidings of good things"*. We can't even speak of His glorious accomplishments and His amazing blessings to us without feeling we need to tag on a condition. **We don't want the sheep to think that grace is cheap, so we make them *pay* for it. We don't want them to get lazy, so we put them to work.**

When we view our spiritual practices as something other than the *fruit* of what *He* has accomplished and begin to see our traditions as the *means* by which *we* perfect what He has done, we are living under a mixture of law and grace. This is the same as saying that when Jesus said, "It is finished," He really meant, "It is only just begun"—that His redemption was enough to save us, but in order to be kept until the day of ultimate salvation, *we* must complete certain religious practices. **It is "another" gospel to reason that Jesus died and rose again to make us only *capable* of**

obeying the law instead of teaching that we are new creations completely free from it.

Jesus *died* to set us free from law and *give* us grace. Grace isn't cheap, but it *is* absolutely free. That's the point. All of the marvels that are ours are *received* as a gift purchased for us with *His* blood, not ours.

Day 17

HUNGRY, THIRSTY, AND DESPERATE

*M*any Christians today are seeking to be closer to God and would describe themselves as hungry, thirsty, and even desperate for Him. They have read multiple books on prayer, know all the major prayer formulas, and practice at least one of them regularly, hoping with everything to finally reach that moment when they can sense God's presence deeply and hear Him speak to their hearts. They are determined but never completely satisfied.

Others, when they sense that God is far away, shrug their shoulders and conclude that "this is all there is". Sure, when they first came to Jesus they felt so very close to Him, but now, let's face it; they don't often sense His presence. "So what?" they reason, "I didn't become a Christian for goose-bumps and supernatural experiences. My life is dedicated to Jesus. No matter how I *feel*, I will keep worshipping and serving Him." They are dedicated but mostly miserable.

We've taught formulas for intimacy with God. We and those we've taught have employed them consistently, but instead of God feeling closer, He feels far away. Some are asking God to help them understand why they feel this way. They know they aren't perfect, but they are doing almost everything they think they are supposed to do. They know that God is near, because of what they've learned in the Bible, but if you ask them they will honestly say that He doesn't feel close at all, at least not as He did in the beginning. Or they "sense His presence" now and then, but not moment by moment. They are asking why. They can't think of any unconfessed sin. They are in the ministry or living lives that reflect that they are believers. They want to please God with all of their heart, so why this distance? Why this unsatisfied longing? Where is the love they once knew? Where's the joy? They are confused but still hold out hope that there is an answer to their dilemma.

An increasing number of believers have become desperate and are now taking a more questionable route in their search. In the extreme we see people in some countries offering their bodies to be crucified, whipping themselves until they bleed, or walking on their bare hands and knees for miles to gain God's favor. Most of us would never consider doing such a thing, though some might empathize with the motive behind their efforts. Perhaps most would not go to such extremes, but there are multiple thousands today who are so desperate to once again experience the presence of God that they will scream at the top of their lungs, make animal noises, crawl around like animals, feign miracles in order to "inspire others to believe", or receive "impartations" which cause them to behave like demoniacs. They are desperately deceived.

While I believe that every working of the Holy Spirit available to the Early Church is still ours today, much of what people think is the Holy Spirit is fakery at the very least and I'm sad to say in some cases, this supposed "manifest presence of God" is "other" in nature. Are we to rationalize that if something gives us chills, makes us laugh uncontrollably, overpowers us, electrifies us, or appears to be a supernatural manifestation, it must be from God? We shouldn't.

Matthew 24:23-26
"Then if anyone says to you, 'Look, here is the Christ!' or 'There!' do not believe it. ²⁴ For false christs and false prophets will rise and show great signs and wonders to deceive, if possible, even the elect.

153

²⁵ See, I have told you beforehand. ²⁶ Therefore if they say to you, 'Look, He is in the desert!' do not go out; or 'Look, He is in the inner rooms!' do not believe it.

Certainly, the opinion about when these things will take place varies from one eschatological camp to another, but what we can conclude is that deceptive signs and wonders exist. Even more horrifying is that the *elect* of God *can* be deceived by them. Could there come a time when Christians will be "looking for Jesus" here and there? My observation is that this is already happening. Believers are traveling far distances to "be in the presence of God" or to "experience a refreshing from God" because they've heard His presence is in this church or that place or under a certain person's ministry. Please consider how pitiful this is. Christians—looking for God!

It is not the purpose of this book to debate this topic of what manifestations are or are not of God. What concerns me most is *why*. Why are so many *believers,* even pastors, trying to *find* God? Why are they hungering and thirsting for Him as if they were never born again?

I remember so clearly what happened while sitting in a church we were visiting one Sunday morning several years ago. We were singing a popular song about how we were thirsting and couldn't Jesus please come and fill us. I didn't really think anything of it since this type of song is so common, but the thought came to me, "Never thirst." Knowing this was a scripture, but not remembering all of the words, I asked my husband to hand me his Bible and searched his concordance. I sat stunned as I read these words.

John 6:35
*And Jesus said to them, "I am the bread of life. He who comes to Me shall **never hunger**, and he who believes in Me shall **never thirst**.*

I leaned over and pointed the verse out to my husband, and he raised his eyebrows immediately getting the connection.

There we were, singing about being hungry and thirsty, pleading with God to fill us, but Jesus said we, those who believe in Him, would *never* hunger and *never* thirst. Something obviously was not right with the picture of a room full of believers pleading with God to take away their hunger and thirst. I started wondering what the perspective of a visitor or a child might me. Why would someone want to become a Christian if he is going to feel so desperate? Aren't believers supposed to have the life of Jesus overflowing from them? Where's the joyous contentment we advertise?

I later emailed this revelation to the worship leader of that church, thinking he would also be amazed by my discovery. Instead I got this answer, "As a worship team, *we* have determined that it is important to *cultivate* a hunger and thirst for God among the people." Before continuing, I need to ask this question. Do we do things in ministry because *we* decide it is what is best or do we base what we do on what Scripture teaches us? If we discover we are doing something in error, we need to change, not justify ourselves based on our *opinions*.

In fact, a huge stumbling block in the church today is what I call Consensus Christianity. Instead of making the *Scriptures* our guide, we rely on the agreement between ourselves to speak as truth. Surely we can come to a consensus about truth, but when truth is *defined* by what we have agreed upon together, and it is *not* truth, we deceive ourselves having put our opinions above the written word of God.

The norm should be that we don't hunger and thirst at all. We are supposed to be *satisfied*, walking in a daily sense of fullness. Not only are we supposed to be satisfied but overflowing.

John 4:14
Whoever drinks of the water that I shall give him will ***never*** *thirst. But the water that I shall give him will become in him a* ***fountain*** *of water* ***springing up*** *into everlasting life."*

Remember when we used to proclaim the good news, "Christianity isn't a religion. It's a relationship with Jesus Christ,"? We remember the closeness we felt with God when we first believed in Him. We knew we were forgiven. We knew God was our Father. We knew He loved us so deeply and personally. "Those were the days, my friend. We thought they'd never end,"[47] but gradually, almost without us realizing it, and much to our dismay, they did.

With each other's consent we have become entirely too effective at turning our blessed relationship with God into mere religious practices. We wonder why our new converts gradually lose that joy. In fact, we've come to expect it will happen eventually and we observe their joy with a certain disappointed nostalgia, knowing we used to feel that way— longing to feel that way again, and we are sadly aware that this glorious joy we observe in new believers will one day fade from them as well. After all, it happened to us—most of us unaware of how or why. Not knowing what to do about it and having come to some sort of "peace" with it as to be expected, we just go on preaching the same old same old never considering that there is a *reason* this happens, and the reason is *we* were taught a "gospel" that leads us away from His amazing grace to "another", and we keep passing it on.

---

[47] "Those Were the Days, My Friend", Mary Hopkin

Day 18

ONE SPIRIT

---

*T*here are a variety of reasons believers feel far from God, but in most cases, it is because they are *estranged* from Him. They've fallen from His grace in the true sense of the word. For many years we assumed this verse was talking about those who were involved in sin and thus fallen from grace, and we did not hear what Paul actually said.

Galatians 5:1
Stand fast therefore in the liberty by which Christ has made us free, and do not be entangled again with a yoke of bondage.

We falsely assumed that this "yoke of bondage" was sin when actually it is law. Yet there it was in black and white, but we didn't see it because we heard it preached so many times that it was sin. Yes, we'd read it on our own, even studied it, but when you've heard something one way for a long time, it's as if you can't see what is right in front of your face.

Galatians 5:2-3
*Indeed I, Paul, say to you that if you become circum-cised, Christ will profit you nothing. ³ And I testify again to every man who becomes circumcised that he is a debtor to keep the whole law. ⁴ **You have***

become estranged from Christ, you who attempt to be justified by law; you have fallen from grace.

I believe that this verse is central to determining what it means to preach "another" gospel. Let me explain. See it as a fill-in-the-blank sentence.

You have become estranged from Christ, you who attempt to _____ by following law; you have fallen from grace.

Not just anything can go in the blank for we are dealing with Scripture here. The only words that can go on this line are that which we have been given freely by His grace. For example:

You have become estranged from Christ, you who attempt to _be saved_ (Eph. 2:8-9) by following law; you have fallen from grace.

All of us agree with that one, but try some of these: *forgiven (Col. 2:13), healed (1 Pet. 2:24), be blessed (2 Pet. 1:3, Eph. 1:3), know God (Heb. 8:11), become God's child (Gal. 3:2), go to heaven (Jn. 3:16), be holy (Heb.10:9).* Do you see what I'm trying to demonstrate? These things we receive by grace through faith, not by following laws. I'm confident most of you will agree.

What about this one?

You have become estranged from Christ, you who attempt to _be close to God_ by following law; you have fallen from grace.

Almost instinctively and due to our knowledge of Scripture, something rises up within us and declares, "No, we aren't close to God by following laws. We are close to Him because of the blood of Jesus," (Eph. 2:13, Heb. 10:19).

Exactly.

Nonetheless, it is what is taught—that we *need* to and *can* get close or closer to God through following laws and formulas. It's as if we are suffering from some sort of intellectual disorder that allows us to believe two things that contradict each other—a religious version of "doublethink".[48] We believe with all of our hearts that we have been brought close to God by the blood of Jesus, but at the same time we teach people *how* to get close or closer to God and how to "enter His presence". We've been trained to accept what we call "paradoxes" which cannot possibly be simultaneously true—which cause us to abandon our God-given logic. Only one of these "truths" is really true for if one *needs* to get close or closer to God or to "enter His presence", it means that he is not yet close or close enough or is not in His presence and this means that what Jesus did on the cross was not sufficient to bring us close, and that we need to add to what He did. We teach these conflicting ideas not only in sermons, but in multiple songs which are remembered and recited long after our teachings have been forgotten.

Even worse is our prescription for how to obtain what we already possess, which results in employing certain practices we call "disciplines" and formulas we call "prayer", but in actuality usually become nothing more than law which causes us to feel justified if we follow them and not-quite when we don't, which was my original query—why I felt justified when I prayed and not when I didn't. This brings us back to Paul's warning. When we try to accomplish what we have already been given by grace through faith by following law, we fall from grace for we thus make our relationship no longer based on grace but on a mixture of grace plus law which **nullifies grace entirely**.

---

[48] *1984*, Orwell

The blessed truth, the whole truth, and nothing but the truth is we are as close to God at our new birth as we can ever be.[49]

1 Corinthians 6:17
He who is joined to the Lord is **one spirit with Him.**

We are joined (glued) to the Lord the day we receive Him. We are one spirit with the Living God. That seems simple enough, but let us continue.

---

[49] One person replied to this statement, "I hope I am not as close to God as I will ever be." I believe this is because we have believed the idea that we can get closer through our own efforts which produces an estrangement from Christ, which makes us feel we aren't close, and so we long to be "closer". When we return to the truth that we are already as close to God as we will ever be, then and only then can we rest in His love.

Day 19

HIS PRECIOUS BLOOD

We have been brought as close to God as we can ever be through the blood of His Son. It was *His* sacrifice that caused God to rent the curtain in the temple which separated man from the presence of God, not any sacrifice of ours. God made a way for us to be as close as possible; to enter the holiest place, not via formulas, but through His blood (His grace) and our faith in Jesus Christ.

One of the damaging ways we add the Old into the New when it comes to this topic of our closeness with God, is that of "entering His presence". Here is some more very good news that we need to shout from the mountain tops:

We do not need to enter God's presence for His presence has forever entered us, and we have permanently entered His presence.

Hebrews 6:19-20
*This hope we have as an **anchor** of the soul, both sure and steadfast, and which enters the Presence behind the veil, [20] where the forerunner has entered for us, even Jesus, having become High Priest forever.*
Hebrews 10:19-22
*Therefore, brethren, having boldness to enter the Holiest by the **blood of Jesus**, [20] by a **new** and living way which He consecrated for us, through **the veil**,*

*that is, **His flesh**, [21] and having a High Priest over the house of God, [22] let us draw near with a true heart in full assurance of faith, having our hearts sprinkled from an evil conscience and our bodies washed with pure water.*

When do we enter the Holiest? Our misconception of Hebrews 10:22 causes a common confusion. We forget the message of Hebrews, that the writer is bidding the Jews who had not yet been converted and those who were tempted to return to Judaism, to fully draw near to God without fear, with confidence and not go back to the old way of fearing God's presence (the law). Wuest writes:

This entering into the Holy of Holies which the Messiah inaugurated for sinners was by way of a freshly-slain and living road, and this road went "through the veil, that is to say, His flesh." The inner veil of the tabernacle separated the Holy Place from the Holy of Holies. It barred man's access to God. When the high priest in Israel went into the Holy of Holies, he brushed aside that veil. The writer speaks of Messiah's humanity, as the veil through which the entrance into the heavenly Holy of Holies was made... When the Messiah died on the Cross, the veil of the temple was rent by the unseen hand of God, showing Israel two things, that the Messiah had now provided the actual entrance for the sinner into the presence of God, and that the symbolic sacrifices were to be discontinued, for the Reality to whom they pointed had come (9:7-10).

There is no need for us to go through any formula to "enter God's presence". We are in His presence at all times seated with Him in heavenly places in Christ.

Ephesians 2:4-7
But God, who is rich in mercy, because of His great love with which He loved us, ⁵ even when we were dead in trespasses, made us alive together with Christ (by grace you have been saved), ⁶ and **raised us up together, and made us sit together in the heavenly places in Christ Jesus,** *⁷ that in the ages to come He might show the exceeding riches of His grace in His kindness toward us in Christ Jesus.*

Brothers and sisters, we don't need to "put in our time" in *daily* prayer in order to have the right to pray at *any* time. That may sound shocking to many of you (that someone might believe such a thing), but I actually believed that God would not hear me in time of need if I had not been praying regularly. Can you see the danger of believing such a thing? How could we ever call out to God in time of need if we believe that failing to meet such a standard would cause God to just stand by and watch without coming to our aid? The truth is that God's ears are always open to the prayers of the righteous (who we are by grace through faith). All prayer brings Him joy whether one minute or one hour. He is able and willing to answer all prayer; yes, even if we haven't deliberately prayed for days.

Since we are gloriously and continually cleansed from sin, there is no need to first confess sins before we pray. Sin is no longer separating us from God. He dealt with that on the cross. We are one spirit with Him. We don't need to worship or pray for others first. We simply pray, just as we did when we first came to Him before we heard about even one prayer formula. It is His blood that has placed us permanently in the holiest place, not our daily devotions. God removed the rituals by having His Son become our sacrifice. That sacrifice was good enough to give us a lifetime of closeness with our Father. **He doesn't need us to help out or improve on His work.**

This may all sound too good to be true. Would it hurt to give it a try? Forget the formula and just talk to God. Speak to Him again by grace through faith only, not on the basis of anything you do, but based on His blood alone. Stop thinking about the next time you will "spend time in His presence" and realize that you already are in His presence for His presence is already in you. Then simply stop for a minute and enjoy Him.

Amazingly, not only are we in God's presence and His presence in us, He also promised to be with us as we gather in His name. Even more remarkable is that He promises, without condition, to never leave us or forsake us.

1 John 4:15
*Whoever confesses that Jesus is the Son of God, God **abides** in him, and he in God.*
Colossians 1:27
*To them God willed to make known what are the riches of the glory of this mystery among the Gentiles: which is **Christ in you**, the hope of glory.*
Ephesians 3:17
*That Christ may **dwell** in your hearts through faith.*
John 14:16-17
*And I will pray the Father, and He will give you another Helper, that He may **abide with you for-ever**— [17] the Spirit of truth, whom the world cannot receive, because it neither sees Him nor knows Him; but you know Him, for He dwells with you and will be in you.*
Matthew 18:19-20
*"Again I say to you that if two of you agree on earth concerning anything that they ask, it will be done for them by My Father in heaven. [20] For where two or three are gathered together in My name, **I am there** in the midst of them."*

I'm particularly fond of this verse in the Amplified. It reflects the Greek better than the usual translations.

Hebrews 13:5 Amplified

For He [God] Himself has said, I will not in any way fail you nor give you up nor leave you without support. [I will] not, [I will] not, [I will] not in any degree leave you helpless nor forsake nor let [you] down (relax My hold on you)! [Assuredly not!]

Our friend, David Graybiel, often speaks of God not having a "swivel throne". Can you picture a swivel throne? Pretty funny image, right? Well, God doesn't have one. He doesn't turn and look away when we sin. He doesn't get bored and do twirls in his throne until we really show Him how determined we are. He isn't indifferent in our times of need. He has promised to never ever leave us, not ever. Remember, even if we sin, He is with us.

So the anatomy of the deception looks like this. God brings us perfectly close to Him through the blood of His Son. Instead of just believing this and enjoying it, we listen to those who decree that we need to get "closer". If there is "more" of God or we can get "closer" than we gloriously are experiencing at our new birth, we naively get on board. Once we believe this lie—specifically that we *can* get closer which implies that we *need* to get closer, we accept the invented ways to accomplish this task such as "spiritual disciplines" and formula prayer. Our motivations are good, but misguided.

What we should be taught from the beginning of our walk with God is that we *are* close to Him and we should be encouraged to simply enjoy this closeness and appreciate the price that was paid for us to have it. Instead, wanting to "please" God, we begin to unnecessarily plow forward. As the means of this pursuit becomes a requirement, a law, in our minds, we discover that we feel justified when we pray and read the word and not justified when we don't.[50] As

---

[50] Another way I have heard this expressed is that someone believes that if he doesn't pray each morning, the whole day is just horrible, and that when he does pray, things will go well. This is called superstition, my friends.

this goes on and on, we gradually fall from grace until we experience the estrangement Paul explains.

This is exactly what happened to me. **It wasn't intentional; it just automatically took place when I went from praying *because* I had a close relationship with God to seeing prayer and Bible reading as a *means* of maintaining and improving my closeness with God.** Spiritual disciplines became laws to me. As the years went by, I gradually became estranged from Christ, even though I loved Him with all of my heart. I fell from grace, even though I thought I was doing what I was supposed to do. I could not see that I was trying to perfect myself in my flesh by relying on the laws I had set up! I stopped relying on His grace to receive me and began to trust in my formulas, right living, and good works.

Please hear me, and carefully consider these things. We believers are already close to God. **We can't get closer.**[51] He did everything that needed to be done in order for us to be near. We are one Spirit with Him. We can't improve on the cross. He wants us to know and believe that what His Son accomplished was enough and enjoy what He purchased for us. When we do this, we stop hungering and thirsting and begin to once again live satisfied. Then the rivers of living water, which we dammed up with laws and formulas, begin to bubble up again and overflow into everlasting life. Life!

This is the offense of the cross and why Paul and the early Christians were persecuted. Imagine the religious Jews who had worked so diligently to have a relationship with God and to be righteous before Him being told that all of their hard work was rubbish! Imagine being instructed that by simply by *believing,* they were holy, blameless, righteous, and perfectly close to God. From a mindset based on doing, which was the law system, to the teaching that by God's

---

[51] The day I checked my concordance for the words "closer" and "nearer" in relationship to believers was an eye-opening day indeed for I could not find them. We are either close or we are not; which is to say, we are either born again or we are not.

grace through faith in the name of Jesus and His cross they were accepted by God—well, it was beyond unbelievable. It was foolishness!

Don't we have a similar reaction when we hear these grace extremists going on and on about God's favor? Do we see them as simpletons and shallow in their faith, "single message preachers", looking down upon them as if they were ignorant children splashing in the "shallow" waters of God's love instead of going into the "deeper" things of God? Why should they be so happy? Shouldn't they learn the disciplines of prayer, Bible reading, fasting, and service as we have? Shouldn't they "grow up"?

Consider this. What if grace and faith *are* the deep things of God?

1 Corinthians 2:6-16
However, we speak wisdom among those who are mature, yet not the wisdom of this age, nor of the rulers of this age, who are coming to nothing. ⁷ But we speak the wisdom of God in a mystery, the hidden wisdom which God ordained before the ages for our glory, ⁸ which none of the rulers of this age knew; for had they known, they would not have crucified the Lord of glory.

They would not have crucified Him had they known what He would accomplish through His death and resurrection.

⁹ But as it is written:
"Eye has not seen, nor ear heard,
Nor have entered into the heart of man
The things which God has prepared for those who love Him."

We often stop after the above verse as if there is still so much we have to learn—to "go deeper". Yet, the thought continues.

*[10] But God **has revealed** them to us through His Spirit.*

Surprising, isn't it? God already revealed to us the things which He prepared for those who love Him through His Sprit and that happened without our efforts.

*For the Spirit searches all things, yes, **the deep things** of God.[52] [11] For what man knows the things of a man except the spirit of the man which is in him? Even so no one knows the things of God except the Spirit of God. [12] Now we have received, not the spirit of the world, but the Spirit who is from God, that **we might know the things that have been freely given** (graciously given) **to us by God**.*

The Sprit within us searches the deep things of God. Do we even talk that much about the things that have been graciously given to us by God? No, not usually. We focus more on what *we* need to give to God. It's as if we are running interference for that which the Spirit wants to reveal.

[13] These things we also speak, not in words which man's wisdom teaches but which the Holy Spirit teaches, comparing spiritual things with spiritual. [14] But the natural man does not receive the things of the Spirit of God, for they are foolishness to him; nor can he know them, because they are spiritually discerned.

The natural man is the non-believer. The non-believer cannot comprehend these mysteries. In fact, he sees them as foolishness. Blood removing sin? That's ridiculous. Being made righteous apart from works? Unthinkable! Offensive!

---

[52] Notice, the passage says that God already revealed these deep things of God to us, and if that isn't convincing enough, he continues in verse 12 stating that we "freely" know the deep things of God—and yes, that the deep things of God are what He's freely **given** to us.

*¹⁵ But he who is spiritual judges all things, yet he himself is rightly judged by no one. ¹⁶ For "who has known the mind of the LORD that he may instruct Him?" But we **have** the mind of Christ.*

Dearly beloved of God, we *have* the mind of Christ. All believers have the mind of Christ. The Spirit of God reveals to us the deep things of God so that we may know what we have been freely **given** by God: eternal salvation, everlasting life, perfect forgiveness, the righteousness of God, peace with God, holiness, blamelessness, every spiritual blessing in the heavenly places in Christ Jesus, all things pertaining to life and godliness, being made partakers of the divine nature, dead to the law, alive in Christ, living in His presence, having His presence live in us, provision, healing, spiritual gifts, heirs of God, co-heirs with Christ, sons and daughters of God, accepted in the Beloved.

All of these things and more are ours!

Day 20

IF YOU WILL ONLY

*T*hree years ago, I had an experience which, quite frankly, surprised me. David had begun a series in Ephesians and was finishing up teaching Chapter 2 by reviewing both chapters. He listed one thing after another that God accomplished in Christ. The list was amazing enough, but he finished his sermon by saying, "And all these things are YOURS!"

Even after many years of learning and believing and knowing deep in my heart that all of those things are mine by grace through faith alone as a gift from God, I caught my mind adding, "...if *you* will only—" This demonstrated to me the power of "another" gospel; of adding law to grace; or more specifically in this case, that of adding conditions to grace. So accustomed was I to having every blessing of God connected to an action of mine, that even after all of those years of knowing better, I was waiting for the boom to be lowered. I sat their stunned with my mouth open, amazed that the idea of earned provision still lurked in the back of my mind and again rejoicing that all of these things are indeed ours as a gift from God not based on anything we do, but on what Jesus Himself accomplished.

Why is it so difficult for us to *receive* gifts from God? Why do we keep insisting that we must "do our part" (pay) in order to receive them, maintain them, or improve them?

Part of this is due to the world in which we live, one that is based on our basic recipe for success: work hard and receive what we deserve/earn for our labors. As children we "behave" at home and receive rewards from our parents, and if we disobey, we are punished. Why, even Santa gives to us based on whether we are "naughty or nice"! We study diligently in college and earn good grades and eventually a degree. We work hard at our jobs and merit a raise and a promotion for our faithfulness. We greatly admire someone who "pulls himself up by the boot straps". We do good things for others expecting that they will return the favor. We follow the laws and stay out of jail. There's a general societal agreement that when things go wrong, it must in some way, perhaps indirectly, be our fault or we are "getting what we deserve". If good comes to someone we know and love we think, "It couldn't have happened to nicer people." If that boat gets rocked and someone who clearly doesn't deserve a break gets one, we are privately perturbed. Or if something awful happens to someone nice, we are baffled as to why.[53]

Then along comes Jesus announcing glad tidings of good things, "Whoever *believes* in Me will not perish, but have everlasting life."

"Believe" means, of course, "to have faith".[54] By God's grace through faith we receive everything Jesus died to accomplish. We cannot earn these things, because they are gifts. We can only receive them. If we could work for them,

---

[53] The question isn't, "Why do bad things happen to good people?" but rather, "Why do bad things happen?" for bad things happen to all. The world is fallen, full of disease, driven by evil forces, and affected by people making wrong choices. That is why bad things happen. Consider this seldom asked question, "Why do good things happen?" Good things happen to all because God causes the sun to rise and the rain to fall (both blessings) on all people. "Every good and perfect gift" comes from Him and there are many who are His who do His will which is to love others. This is why good things happen to all.

[54] In English, we don't have a verb for faith (i.e. "faithing"). The verb for faith is believe. To have faith = to believe; faith = belief. Keeping this in mind helps us to better understand "faith".

then they would cease to be gifts and be wages instead, something we deserve.

Romans 4:4-5
Now to him who works, the wages are not counted as grace but as debt. [5] *But to him who does not work but **believes** on Him who justifies the **ungodly**, his **faith** is accounted for righteousness.*

Christianity is the *only* religion based on God's grace. All other religions are based on what the individual does and the hope that their diligent efforts will someday pay off.

What Christ did was good enough. We need not and cannot add to it. It needn't be "balanced" with our own labors.[55] Everything we have and everything we are is a gift to us by grace alone through faith in Him alone. This is contrary to all the principles of the world, and it offends the religious mind to its core! It goes against all religions, and I'm sad to say, it goes against the prevailing teachings in the "Christian" church today.

How long will we continue to adopt the world's system of "work hard and be rewarded" instead of embracing what only God could have designed—a relationship with Him based on His grace alone received by human beings who can *never* be good enough and *never* do enough good to deserve it and thus must rely solely on faith in the grace of God to receive it?

We need to wake up and see that our relationship with God is already as good as God declares it to be. We need to realize that there is a reason we have this sense we can never be good enough. It's because we can't have a relationship with God in our own power or through our own discipline, let alone "deserve" one. Our closeness with God and everything we receive from Him is based solely on what Jesus did, not on what we do. This is the rest we were promised. It is why our yoke is "easy" and our burden is "light".

---

[55] We do good works BECAUSE of what we've been given, not to obtain.

Let these truths sink into your heart. There is nothing we can do to make ourselves holy and righteous before the living God that would ever be good enough. Only by His grace through faith in His Son can we ever be what we are needlessly trying to become. We must cease from our labors and enter His rest. When we finally do, we find again the joy of our salvation. We rediscover our first love. We are able to breathe in and enjoy this LIFE He promised, and the fruit that we previously worked so hard to produce will simply happen. Sin that might be tormenting us will drop like scales as it did in the beginning of our walk. When we finally understand that "It is finished!" we can stop wasting our time and energy trying to accomplish what we've already been given and finally be free from, "If you will only..."

Day 21

HEALTHY SHEEP

*A*ll true shepherds work diligently so that their sheep will be healthy. It's not that they don't care. The problem is most shepherds today are using law and formula instead of grace and faith to guide the flock. The "results" look similar, but the sheep living under law are oppressed, miserable, self-righteous, and self-focused sheep who constantly have to be led and coached by the pastor; whereas, the sheep who are being fed the gospel of God's grace are free, joyful, and Jesus-focused sheep who know their righteousness is a gift and who are led by the Spirit.

Upon reawakening to God's amazing grace we were faced with the fact that our belief system and what we taught was nearly all law-based. That is to say, we taught what *we and the sheep* needed to do to be holy, live righteously, know God, get closer to God, and we put a heavy emphasis on spiritual warfare; which, of course in our thinking, was all about *our* efforts. As one pastor we know who was also reawakening to grace put it, "Everything I've been teaching is all wrong," and this was certainly true for us.

Not all ministers can handle this realization so gracefully. It seems only natural that some ministers today would have a strong reaction about the possibility that they might be teaching an anti-gospel[56] message. There can be significant

---

[56] Dare I say, "anti-Christ"?

ego wrapped around the hundreds of files of sermons we have labored so diligently to produce. Add that to years of laboring arduously to bring about revival, and a sort of resistance can arise. When one's entire life has been spent studying and sharing a certain message, one becomes completely confident of it as if repeating the same thing eventually makes it true. Imagine how the Pharisees and Scribes felt. They had the Scriptures memorized, followed them meticulously, and taught them continually. Jesus came along challenging them and seemingly adding to them saying, "You have heard that it was said..., but I say unto you..." Then after His death His disciples declared that the Covenant they treasured so dearly and wanted to preserve was obsolete!

Thankfully, many respond to this call for a return to the pure gospel of grace as did the Pharisee Saul when confronted with the truth about Jesus Christ. He had his religious pedigree in perfect order. It brought him status among his associates. He was respected and admired and even honored. According to the righteousness that was in the law, he declared that he was blameless (Phil. 3:6). Imagine that! Yet, when Paul was confronted with the grace of God, he laid it all aside to gain Christ and be found in Him, not having a righteousness based on keeping the law, but one based on simply believing in Jesus. He gave up everything for the truth of the gospel.

Also, consider Peter's humble response when he was rebuked by Paul for withdrawing from eating with the Gentiles when the Jewish brothers arrived. In doing this Paul wrote that Peter was "not straightforward about the truth of the gospel" (Gal. 2:14). Compared to Peter who was there with Jesus from the beginning, Paul would seem to have no business correcting him, but Paul knew that Peter's actions were preaching "another" gospel—shouting to all present that the Gentiles were not quite clean enough because they were not circumcised and didn't follow dietary laws. Yet in Peter's epistle, he referred to Paul as "our beloved brother,

Paul". Certainly, he had no animosity toward the one who had publicly rebuked him.

My question is can we do the same? Will we let go of our accomplishments and religious status among our peers, possibly facing rejection and persecution by friends and family, and return to grace-through-faith-righteousness? Can we, like Apollos, receive correction from the voices that are rising? Or will we simply give a nod to grace, preach a couple sermons about it, perhaps even with the intent to suppress it, and then go back to putting new wine into old wine skins?

God's sheep deserve better than that. They deserve to hear the glad tidings of good things; the truth, the whole truth, and nothing but the truth. Don't we have sufficient teaching material about the beauty and wonder of God in the pages of Scripture to last a lifetime? **Why are so many of us teaching what to *do* instead of what to *believe*** (Rom. 10:5-13)? Shouldn't we magnify what Jesus accomplished *for* us through his death and resurrection?

1 Corinthians 1:30-32 NASB
*But by **His** doing you are in Christ Jesus, who **became to us** wisdom from God, and righteousness and sanctification, and redemption, ³¹ so that, just as it is written, "LET HIM WHO BOASTS, BOAST IN THE LORD."*

We need to feed the sheep continually with what *He* did and who we are *in Him*. We need to boast in *His* accomplishments, not continually emphasize the need for ours. The focus needs to be on Jesus and not on us!

Why are we telling sheep to die, when they already died with Christ (Col. 3:3)? All that amounts to is false humility (Col. 2:23). Shouldn't we be teaching them what it means to live (Jn. 3:16, Gal. 2:20)? Why do we keep telling believers that they are "only sinners saved by grace" when the Bible teaches us that we *were* sinners, but now we are righteous (Rom. 5:19, 1 Tim. 1:9)? We were unholy, but now we are saints (Col.1:21-22). These truths should be shouted from

176

the mountain tops as Christ's greatest accomplishments! Instead of telling people that they need to stop sinning, why not show them that they died to and are free from sin (Rom. 6)? This is the *good* news. We need to stop beating the sheep with law after law after law and instead strengthen them with grace upon grace and more grace (Jn. 1:16).

Day 22

THE WORD OF GOD

---

*O*ver the centuries, the church has lost its understanding of the term "word of God". Most understand "the word of God" to refer to the written word of God and others see it also as the spoken word of God, but the truth is that the term "word of God" most commonly refers to the gospel. [57] Please allow me to share a few scriptures that demonstrate this truth.

When Samaria "received the word of God" it meant only one thing. They heard the gospel of Jesus Christ and received it—they were born again.

Acts 8:4-6, 12, 14-17 NASB
*Therefore, those who had been scattered went about **preaching the word**. [5] Philip went down to the city of Samaria and began **proclaiming Christi***

---

[57] I'm not one who makes a distinction between "logos" and "rhema" having once done a lengthy study of the two which caused me to conclude that they are used synonymously. I mention this only because what I'm about to say has nothing to do with the distinctions some have made. I did not catalog my study, but others who have come to the same conclusion have recorded their results; for example, William G. Dicks in an article entitled "The WORD of God: RHEMA vs. LOGOS–Its meaning and uses" gives a detailed view of the uses of rhema and logos.

*to them. ⁶ The crowds with one accord were giving attention to what was said by Philip, as they heard and saw the signs which he was performing. ⁷ For in the case of many who had unclean spirits, they were coming out of them shouting with a loud voice; and many who had been paralyzed and lame were healed. ⁸ So there was much rejoicing in that city.¹² But when they believed Philip **preaching the good news** about the kingdom of God and the name of Jesus Christ, they were being baptized, men and women alike. ¹⁴ Now when the apostles in Jerusalem heard that Samaria had received **the word of God**, they sent them Peter and John, ¹⁵ who came down and prayed for them that they might receive the Holy Spirit. ¹⁶ For He had not yet fallen upon any of them; they had simply been baptized in the name of the Lord Jesus. ¹⁷ Then they began laying their hands on them, and they were receiving the Holy Spirit.*

After Peter was given a vision about not calling what God deems holy as unclean, he went where no Jew dared to go, to the home of Cornelius, a Gentile, and shared the gospel with them (Acts 10). To Peter's amazement, Cornelius and the other Gentiles assembled with him received the gospel and were also saved. Notice how this is recorded. The "word of God" clearly here is referring to the good news about Jesus.

Acts 11:1
*Now the apostles and brethren who were in Judea heard that the Gentiles had also received **the word of God**.*

This verse is obviously not talking about a written document, but the gospel being received by the lost. The gospel is alive. It is the power of God unto salvation.

Acts 12:24
*But **the word of God** grew and multiplied.*

The Scriptures were preeminent in Jewish synagogues. Although the Early Church used the Law and Prophets to demonstrate that Jesus was the Christ, the "word of God" they preached was the good news about the Messiah.

Acts 13:5
*And when they arrived in Salamis, **they preached the word of God** in the synagogues of the Jews.*

Clearly, we are not born again by the Bible or by reading the Bible. We are born again by grace through faith in Jesus—the good news.

1 Peter 1:23
*Having been born again, not of corruptible seed but incorruptible, **through the word of God** which lives and abides forever.*

When the Jews rejected the word of God in Antioch, they were rejecting the gospel which could bring them everlasting life. When they refused the word of God, Paul and Barnabas took the message to the Gentiles who instead glorified the word of the Lord, and received eternal life.

Acts 13:46-48
*Then Paul and Barnabas grew bold and said, "It was necessary that **the word of God** should be spoken to you first; but since you reject it, and judge yourselves unworthy of **everlasting life**, behold, we turn to the Gentiles. ⁴⁷ For so the Lord has commanded us: 'I have set you as a light to the Gentiles, That you should be for **salvation** to the ends of the earth.'"*

180

*⁴⁸ Now when the Gentiles heard this, they were glad and glorified **the word of the Lord**. And as many as had been appointed to **eternal life** believed.*

When understood in context, the word of God in the next passage is referring to the gospel, the glad tidings of good things.

Romans 10:14-17
How then shall they call on Him in whom they have not believed? And how shall they believe in Him of whom they have not heard? And how shall they hear without a preacher? ¹⁵ And how shall they preach unless they are sent? As it is written:
*"How beautiful are the feet of those who preach **the gospel of peace**,*
*Who bring **glad tidings of good things!**"*
*¹⁶ But they have not all obeyed **the gospel**.*
For Isaiah says, "LORD, who has believed our report?"
¹⁷ So then faith comes by hearing, and hearing by the word of God (the word of Christ). [58]

It would be foolish to declare that every instance of "the word of God" in the New Testament refers only to the gospel, but we must admit that clearly it does so predominantly. When we begin to see this, we can more clearly grasp the meaning of other passages that heretofore we have misinterpreted to mean "Scripture" or "the Bible". Here are some examples. Notice the obvious contextual correlation to salvation.

Luke 8:11-12
*"Now the parable is this: **The seed is the word of God** (the gospel). ¹² Those by the wayside are the ones who hear; then the devil comes and takes away*

---
[58] NASB

*the word out of their hearts, lest they should **believe
and be saved**.*

Acts 6:4

*But we will give ourselves continually to prayer and
to **the ministry of the word** (the gospel).*

2 Corinthians 2:15-17

*For we are to God the fragrance of Christ among
those who are **being saved** and among those who
are perishing. ¹⁶ To the one we are the aroma of
death leading to death, and to the other the aroma
of life **leading to life**. And who is sufficient for these
things? ¹⁷ For we are not, as so many, **peddling the
word of God** (the gospel); but as of sincerity, but as
from God, we **speak** in the sight of God in Christ.*

Ephesians 6:17

*And take the helmet of **salvation**, and the sword of
the Spirit, which is **the word of God** (the gospel).*

2 Corinthians 4:1-4

*Therefore, since we have this ministry, as we have
received mercy, we do not lose heart. ² But we have
renounced the hidden things of shame, not walking
in craftiness nor handling **the word of God** (the
gospel) deceitfully, but by manifestation of the truth
commending ourselves to every man's conscience
in the sight of God. ³ But even if our gospel is veiled,
it is veiled to those who are perishing, ⁴ whose minds
the god of this age has blinded, who do not believe,
lest the light of the **gospel** of the glory of Christ, who
is the image of God, should shine on them.*

1 Timothy 4:4

*For every creature of God is good, and nothing is to
be refused if it is received with thanksgiving; ⁵ for it
is sanctified by the **word of God** (the gospel is what
declares all foods clean) and prayer.*

Hebrews 4:12

*For **the word of God** (the gospel) is living and
powerful, and sharper than any two-edged sword,
piercing even to the division of soul and spirit, and of*

joints and marrow, and is a discerner of the thoughts and intents of the heart.

Each and every time we teach "the word of God" we need to remember that the word of God is the gospel and that the gospel is of God's grace (Acts 20:24). Grace *is* the gospel, the glad tidings of good things. Grace is for the lost. Grace is for the saved. The grace of God, the gospel, cannot be balanced with anything. It is far too amazing to be balanced.

Romans 1:16-17
*For I am not ashamed of the **gospel** of Christ, for it is the **power** (dunamis) of God to salvation for everyone who believes, for the Jew first and also for the Greek. [17] For in it the righteousness of God is revealed from faith to faith; as it is written, "The just shall live by faith."*

Day 23

TWO GREAT COMMANDS

---

*I*n his insightful book, <u>Love Revolution: Rediscovering the Lost Command of Jesus</u>, Gaylord Enns catalogs his discovery of a mixture of covenants that few have pointed out before him. So radical was his realization that some have rejected it out-of-hand. Yet, understanding this revelation is core to comprehending how great the accomplishments of the cross truly are.

Before reading his book my understanding of Matthew 22:37-40 was that loving God with our entire being and loving our neighbor as ourselves would cover all of God's will and the doing of them would be to please God. Having read the gospels at a very young age, I was also very keenly aware of Christ's command to love one another as He loved us. Seeing no conflict, I simply merged the three together as the core commands pertaining to the Christian life.

One afternoon, as we were leaving an out-of-town store we'd visited to purchase items for our daughter's engagement party, someone called out to me from a car window. I didn't recognize our former pastor and his wife at first, but when I did, I went to our car to get David. Patti and Gaylord were visiting in a nearby town where he had gone to get away to work on the aforementioned book. They were looking for a certain shopping center which Gaylord assured Patti he could locate. Finally realizing that they were lost, he told her that he would ask for directions from the next person he saw. Imagine their surprise when the next person they saw was me. Understanding the amazing "coincidence" of us all meeting this way after so many years of not seeing each other, we decided to sit down in a nearby café.

We thought, of course, that this might be an opportunity for *us* to share with them about what God was teaching us about grace. Yet it was Gaylord who began first asking us, "What are the two great commands of the New Covenant?" My husband's first reaction was to buckle. He didn't believe we were under any laws. Not knowing how to answer the question, David gave the answer he thought Gaylord wanted to hear and that was, of course, to love God completely and our neighbor as ourselves. Then Gaylord began to speak of the command of Christ to love one another as He loved us as being the core command of the New Covenant.

To fully understand the import of Matthew 22:37-40, we need only apply basic hermeneutics. To whom was Jesus speaking and about what?

Matthew 22:34-40

*But when the **Pharisees** heard that He had silenced the Sadducees, they gathered together. ³⁵ Then one of them, a lawyer, asked Him a question, testing Him, and saying, ³⁶ "Teacher, which is the great commandment **in the law**?"*
*³⁷ Jesus said to him, "'You shall love the Lord your God with all your heart, with all your soul, and with all your mind.' ³⁸ This is the first and great commandment. ³⁹ And the second is like it: 'You shall love your neighbor as yourself.' ⁴⁰ On these two commandments hang **all the Law and the Prophets**."*

Jesus was speaking to the Pharisees specifically about the greatest commandments in the **law**, the Old Covenant.[59] On these commandments depend all of the law

---

[59] Again, allow me to point out the obvious, that even Jesus considered the law to include the moral law.

and Prophets. Beloved, the question is specific to the Old Covenant and the Old Covenant, as we know, is obsolete.

The necessity of these Old Covenant commandments point to two undeniable facts: One, the Israelites *needed* to be **commanded** to love God and to love their neighbor as themselves because two, it was not in their unredeemed natures to do so. Consider this also, that even though the Israelites were commanded to love God and their neighbors, we read time and time again of their failure to do either.

Romans 8:2-4
*For the law of the Spirit of life in Christ Jesus has made me free from the law of sin and death. ³ **For what the law could not do in that it was weak** through the flesh, God did by sending His own Son in the likeness of sinful flesh, on account of sin: He condemned sin in the flesh, ⁴ that the righteous requirement of the law might be fulfilled in us who do not walk according to the flesh but according to the Spirit.*

The command to love God was an Old Covenant command necessary for a stiff-necked people who were still dead in their sin. The law could not change the heart, only demand the commanded behavior and reveal man's depravity.

We, however, are new creations in Christ Jesus; those who love God because we are loved by Him (1 John 4:19). No one has to command believers to love God. We do. He is our Father, and we are His beloved children. For those who have been born again it is our new nature to love God.

Romans 8:28
And we know that all things work together for good to those who love God, to those who are the called according to His purpose.

Believers are "the called according to His purpose". *We* are "those who love God".

186

On the night of His betrayal, when Jesus spoke of the New Covenant in His blood, He gave them a "new commandment" which He called His own. It was on this commandment to "love one another as I have loved you" (Jn. 13:34-35) and the Father's commandment to believe in the Son (Jn. 6:29), that the entire New Covenant is based.

John 3:23
*And this is His commandment: that we should **believe** on the name of His Son Jesus Christ and **love one another**, as He gave us commandment.*

Believe in Jesus, and love each other as He loved us. When we do these two things we will be keeping His commandments. It's really not that complicated.

Those who love God will love each other. (Please note: I am not telling you to prove that you love God by loving each other. I'm saying that if you are a believer—one who loves God, you *will* love each other.)

1 John 4:7-8
Beloved, let us love one another, for love is of God; and everyone who loves is born of God and knows God. [8] He who does not love does not know God, for God is love.
1 Thessalonians 4:9
But concerning brotherly love you have no need that I should write to you, for you yourselves are taught by God to love one another.

Even more stunning is the understanding that when we love each other, God receives it as love for Himself.

Matthew 25:40
"And the King will answer and say to them, 'Assuredly, I say to you, inasmuch as you did it to one of the least of these My brethren, you did it to Me.'"

John 21:17

He said to him the third time, "Simon, son of Jonah, do you love Me?" Peter was grieved because He said to him the third time, "Do you love Me?" And he said to Him, "Lord, You know all things; You know that I love You." Jesus said to him, "Feed My sheep."

Have you ever considered just how much love a pastor demonstrates for God when he shows kindness toward his sheep? Every sermon taught, every act of kindness shown is an act of love toward God. This is *God's* perspective. He receives our love toward each other as love toward Him.

Recently, I took my granddaughter, Emma, on a clothing shopping spree to celebrate with her that she had been accepted into the school of her choice. She and I had such a great time picking out a mini wardrobe, and my daughter told me that when she got home, Emma laid out her clothes across her bed to show her mom. I was so happy to do this for her, and she was so happy to receive, but there was another person who was in on this love, and that was my daughter, Christina. She received my love for my granddaughter as love for her. I believe this is a snapshot of how God views our love for His children. When we lavish grace on each other, it brings Him joy.

It's so easy for those who are trying to love God with all of their being to see loving each other as something less important than "loving God", but we need to recognize that **Jesus** *commands* us to love each other as He loved us. By believing on His Son and loving each other, we bring pleasure to the Father's heart. Can the Christian life really be this restful?

Yes!

Day 24

TO LOVE OR BE LOVED

While the Old Covenant commanded Israel to love God, the New Covenant emphasizes how much God loves us! Even in commanding us to love each other, Jesus explains in what manner we are to love, adding "as I have loved you." We spend so much time and energy trying to prove our love for God through carrying out our long list of spiritual disciplines that we seldom take time to recognize how deeply He loves us. Yet Scripture clearly teaches us that love is not about *our* love for God, but about *His* love for us.

> *1 John 4:10*
> *In this is love, **not** that we loved God, but that **He** loved us and sent His Son to be the propitiation for our sins.*

In some cases we even minimize the importance of God's love for us with some sort of twisted idea that highlighting His love for *us* is to become self-focused or shallow. "Let us move on to the deeper things of God," we often hear.

Please tell me, if anyone can, is there something more important, something deeper than God's love for us?

Ephesians 3:14-19
*For this reason I bow my knees to the Father of our Lord Jesus Christ, ¹⁵ from whom the whole family in heaven and earth is named, ¹⁶ that He would grant you, according to the riches of His glory, to be strengthened with might through His Spirit in the inner man, ¹⁷ that Christ may dwell in your hearts through faith; **that you, being rooted and grounded in love, ¹⁸ may be able to comprehend with all the saints what is the width and length and depth and height— ¹⁹ to know the love of Christ which passes knowledge; that you may be filled with all the fullness of God.***

God *wants* us to realize how immensely He loves us! When we know and believe how deeply we are loved, we are filled with all of His fullness, and those rivers of living water begin to overflow. How could anything be more marvelous than knowing we are loved by the living God?

This Covenant is not about us. It's about Jesus. The Old Covenant was between God and the Children of Israel. This New Covenant is between the Father and the Son. Just as God caused Abram to fall into a deep sleep so that the covenant He made with him would be an everlasting covenant which would not be dependent upon Abram keeping it, so God has taken us out of the way so that we are not able to break His covenant. It's not about us and what *we* do. It's about Jesus and what *He* did to show His love for us. It's not about loving God with all of our heart, soul, mind, body, and strength in order to demonstrate our love for God. It's about Him giving his heart, soul, mind, body, and strength to demonstrate His love for us (Rom. 5:8). He simply asks us to receive this love and then love each other.

We need to remind ourselves of this basic truth: God loved us when we were His enemies, before we did one single thing to show our love for Him. Thus, His love for us is initially and forever completely undeserved.

Romans 5:6-10

For when we were still without strength, in due time Christ died for the ungodly. [7] For scarcely for a righteous man will one die; yet perhaps for a good man someone would even dare to die. [8] **But God demonstrates His own love toward us, in that while we were still sinners, Christ died for us.** *[9] Much more then, having now been justified by His blood, we shall be saved from wrath through Him. [10] For if when we were enemies we were reconciled to God through the death of His Son, much more, having been reconciled, we shall be saved by His life.*

Notice that the word "demonstrates"[60] is in the present tense. His own love for us is continually shown to us through the fact that while we were still sinners, Christ died for us.[61] What were we doing that would be worthy of meriting God's love before believing in Him? Nothing! **This equation does not change after we become Christians.** In fact, it appears that His love for us even intensifies saying that "much more now" having been justified (made righteous) by His blood, we will also be saved from wrath through Him. We were reconciled through the death of His Son, but now we are saved by His life—the very life that resides within us.

Being reconciled to God means we are at peace, not war, with Him. We do not need to fear His wrath. We are no longer enemies. We are friends. He is our Father. We are His beloved children.

Romans 5:1-2

Therefore, having been justified by **faith,** *we have* **peace** *with God through our Lord Jesus Christ, [2] through whom also we have access by faith into*

---

[60] "Demonstrates" means commends, presents as worthy.

[61] I would be amiss not to note that this passage clearly states that we "were" sinners.

*this **grace** in which we stand, and rejoice in hope of the glory of God.*
Romans 8:15-17
*For you did not receive the spirit of bondage again to **fear**, but you received the Spirit of adoption by whom we cry out, "Abba, Father."* [16] ***The Spirit Himself bears witness with our spirit that we are children of God,*** [17] *and if children, then heirs—heirs of God and joint heirs with Christ, if indeed we suffer with Him, that we may also be glorified together.*

This insidious indoctrination that devalues God's love for us and our position as His beloved children begins almost immediately.

I so clearly remember one day very early into my adult walk with God, still a teenager, being overtaken with joy realizing the fact that God, Creator of heaven and earth, was my Father. As I walked along my way to a downtown coffeehouse outreach that our church sponsored, I began to compose a very sweet song.

My Father made this world
And everything in it!
My God made you and He made me.
He gave His only Son
To purchase my pardon
He gave his life to set me free!

It was pretty exhilarating to have this lovely melody rise up in my heart accompanied by the precious knowledge of God's greatness and love for me, so I didn't hesitate to share my burgeoning composition with an "older" brother in the Lord who worked there, thinking that he would be blessed by it, too. I will never forget his response. He seemed pretty unimpressed and even *annoyed* by my fanciful lyrics and said, "Why don't you write a song about picking up your cross and dying with Jesus?" So innocent was I, and so eager to please, that I changed my song right there on the spot to:

Pick up your cross and die with me
You will also rise again with me.
Lay down your life and lose it.
You will also gain it one day.
He who seeks to save His life
Will lose it one day,
But He who forsakes all will gain.

Certainly, when we come to Christ, we die and then rise with Him, but can you see my point about the immediate programming that diminishes the wonders of God's love for us? This fellow was not amused that I was actually basking in the joy of God's love and our relationship as Father and daughter, so he saw to it that my joy was *squelched*. I never finished the first song in favor of the second, and was even asked to sing the altered version for our church. It was my reward for conformity and, sadly, it began to eat away at my awareness of God's love for me.

1 John 3:1-3
Behold *what manner of love the Father has bestowed on us,* ***that we should be called chil-dren of God!*** *Therefore the world does not know us, because it did not know Him.* *² Beloved, now we are children of God; and it has not yet been revealed what we shall be, but we know that when He is revealed, we shall be like Him, for we shall see Him as He is.* *³ And everyone who has this hope in Him purifies himself, just as He is pure.*

The God who created everything loves you. Yes, you personally. His love isn't some cosmic blanket thrown over all, but is extended to each and every individual. His love isn't measured out to you based on your degree of faith-fulness and obedience. Just as the prodigal son's father continued to love him and welcomed him with open arms when he returned, so your Father loves you no matter what sin you are battling or how small your perception of your contribution to His kingdom may be. **You are His child and His love for you is not based on your productivity.**

While it is *common* for a Christian to doubt that God loves him, it is not *normal*. If you're not aware His love, there is a *reason*. God *wants* you to experience His love and His presence. Don't skip over these thoughts rationalizing that it's not important or that it's "just the way it is". Ask God to show you why. He will.

We often think of the words written to the Ephesians about leaving their first love.[62] We assume that their love *for* God had waned; yet, contextually, this makes no sense, for they were zealous for God in every way. Read this passage noticing how diligent they showed their love for God.

Revelation 2:1-4

"To the angel of the church of Ephesus write,
'These things says He who holds the seven stars in His right hand, who walks in the midst of the seven golden lampstands: [2] *"I know your* **works**, *your* **labor**, *your* **patience**, *and that you* **cannot bear those who are evil**. *And you have* **tested those who say they are apostles and are not, and have found them liars;* [3] *and you have* **persevered** *and have* **patience**, *and have* **labored for My name's sake** *and* **have not become weary**. [4] *Nevertheless I have this against you, that you have left your first love.*

Given the church's current understanding of "first love" being that of us "giving our all" to please our Lord, it sure does seem to me that the Ephesians would be a glowing

---

[62] Whether this is the Ephesian church of John's time or an end time church yet to come seems irrelevant to me. They had lost their first love, and the same things can happen to us.

example to any church of loving God with all of their hearts, souls, minds, and strength. In what way were they not pleasing God? It seems that God was entirely pleased with how they were living and serving Him. Could it be that because we have missed the fact that the New Covenant is based on God loving *us*, that we have misinterpreted what it means to leave one's first love? Isn't our first love the knowledge of *His* love, the joy of knowing we are loved by *Him*—our relationship vs. religion understanding? All of us remember that joy of coming to Jesus "just as I am without one plea, but that Thy blood was shed for me."[63] We can almost feel the exhilaration of knowing we were forgiven and accepted in the Beloved. How thankful we were! How overwhelming was our sense of His love. Friends, that is the love the church has left, our first love—that of knowing we are loved by God and simply believing and receiving it.

We work so hard to please God, just as did the Ephesians, and God appreciates all our hard work, but He has something against us, something so powerful that he said to the Ephesians if they didn't return to it, he was going to remove their lampstand. I dare say that I believe God is speaking to many churches and many individuals today. We have labored and demonstrated our love for God, **but have sidelined His love for us.**

God loves us. Glory, glory, hallelujah! He is demonstrating His love to us; not through angel feathers and gold dust, but by giving His Son to die for us. His sacrifice is continually shouting from Calvary, "I love you! I love you! I love you!" God wants a relationship with you—a living *loving* relationship with you. Just like a parent who delights in his child playing with a gift he has received, **God wants you to enjoy *everything* that His precious Son died to give you.** He wants to graciously give you all things. He wants to do exceedingly abundantly above all that you can ask or think according to the power that is working in you

---

[63] A. H. Brown and Charlotte Elliott, 1835, Public Domain

195

(Eph. 3:20). He wants to pour His love and grace upon you, not only "for a season", but for your entire lifetime, and He wants you to proclaim to His people His unconditional and never-ending love for them by what you teach and how you treat them.

1 John 3:18
My little children, let us not love in word or in tongue, but in deed and in truth.

Let me say this again. We need to understand that being a Christian is not, not, not, about *us* and what *we* do. It's about *Jesus* and what *He* did. Salvation, then, isn't simply where we begin, but how we continue to walk.

Colossians 2:6-10
As you therefore have received Christ Jesus the Lord, so walk in Him, ⁷ rooted and built up in Him and established in the faith (in Him), as you have been taught, abounding in it with thanksgiving. ⁸ Beware lest anyone cheat you through philosophy and empty deceit, according to the tradition of men, according to the basic principles of the world, and not according to Christ. ⁹ For in Him dwells all the fullness of the Godhead bodily; ¹⁰ and you are complete in Him, who is the head of all principality and power.

When we put the focus on ourselves and what we do instead of on Jesus and what He did for us, we leave our first love. It's not that our hard work goes unnoticed by God, but that our hard work is not what He desires most from us. He knows that when we know we are loved, good works will follow, but the good works must not become the focus but remain the fruit. He has made us complete in Him so that we may walk in Him in the same way we received Him—by grace through faith. His love for us is our first love. Our love for God is the fruit of our first love.

This truth came alive recently, when a friend of ours who has been unhealthy for years recently rediscovered the truth of God's love for her. Now, this friend has not been in ministry and scarcely attended church for many years due to the intense physical pain she suffered daily. As she walked into the building where we were having one of our meetings, the pain she'd suffered for so long left her and has not returned. More amazingly, when she realized that God loves her and He isn't asking her to do anything to earn His love, the next desire she expressed was to work with her husband in ministry—from nothing to everything almost instantly. That is the power of knowing we are loved.

Clearly, this is what God desires—to bring us to a place where we are convinced that His love for us and blessings to us are by His grace and not as a result of works. When we finally see His amazing love for us, the works for which we've been created become our desire and our joy (1 Cor. 15:10).

Day 25

DEAD OR ALIVE

---

*T*his brings us to what I believe is an errant emphasis in many churches today—that of our supposed need to "die" as believers. The same scriptures on this topic that used to come to my mind, I'm supposing will also come to yours. In my case I admit that for many years I never "proved all things" on this subject but just went along with the flow. In the back of my mind, though, the idea of needing to put myself to death seemed odd. Hadn't I died with Jesus on the cross? Then again, I would recall the verses speaking of dying, and tell myself, "Well, Jesus *did* tell His disciples to pick up their cross "daily" and Paul wrote that he "died daily". Yet something about the whole concept of daily dying to self, continued to trouble me—the thought of all these believers focusing on trying to die to this, and die to that, and die to the other thing, as if what Jesus did on the cross wasn't quite sufficient a death to cover it all.

When I finally began to study this matter more closely it became clear that Paul did not instruct believers to die. He reminded them that they already died. Even though he said that he "died daily" due to the hardships and persecutions he endured (1 Cor. 15:30-32), he saw himself as *already* crucified. This happens when we are born again.

Galatians 2:20
*I **have been** crucified with Christ; it is no longer I
who **live**, but Christ **lives** in me; and the **life** which I
now **live** in the flesh I **live** by faith in the Son of God,
who loved me and gave Himself for me.*

Now, I ask you to consider this question, was Paul dead
or alive? My first reaction used to be that he was both dead
and alive. I was able to come to this conclusion because I
was trained to simply accept such "paradoxes". This helped
me believe things that were not true alongside of believing
what was true; things such as the fact that His presence
now abides permanently within each believer on the one
hand, and the teaching that we need to "enter His presence"
when we pray on the other. That is completely illogical, but
most Christians today just "accept" that both are true when
it is utterly impossible. Similarly, it does not make sense to
say that someone is both alive and dead. **Did God send His
only Son to give us everlasting life or everlasting death?**
Consider a natural example. Lazarus died. Jesus raised
him from the dead. So, after he was raised, was he dead or
alive? Obviously, he was alive. It's the same for us. We died
with Christ, but now we live.[64]
Notice that Paul's emphasis in Galatians 2:20 was on the
life he **lived**. He states that he *had been* crucified making
no mention of needing to die again—that had already happened when he was born again.
We died and were buried with Jesus (Col.2:12). We were
resurrected with Him and even ascended with Him (Col.
2:12-13, Eph. 2:5-6). We are no longer dead. We are alive.
Just as Jesus is no longer dead and buried, neither are we.

---

[64] At first this seems to be a needless semantic argument, but I'm of the
opinion that words really matter. Yes, my old person is dead, but I am
no longer that person. I am a new creation, and I am alive.

Romans 6:5-11
*For if we have been united together in the likeness of His death, certainly we also shall be in the likeness of His resurrection, ⁶ knowing this, that **our old man was crucified with Him**, that the body of sin might be **done away with**, that we should no longer be slaves of sin. ⁷ For he who **has** died has been freed from sin. ⁸ Now if we **died** with Christ, we believe that we shall also **live** with Him, ⁹ knowing that Christ, having been raised from the dead, **dies no more**. Death no longer has dominion over Him. ¹⁰ For the death that He died, He died to sin **once for all**; but the life that He lives, He lives to God. ¹¹ **Likewise (in the same way—just as Jesus died one time but is now alive) you also**, reckon yourselves to be dead indeed to sin, but **alive** to God in Christ Jesus our Lord.*

Our **old** man—the person we **were**—the person who **was** both a sinner and controlled by sinful passions—that person DIED. In the same way that Jesus died **one time** but now lives to God, we also died one time with Him and now LIVE to God—as new creations.

Here is a scripture that gets taken out of context and is used to show that we need to die.

Colossians 3:5-6
*Therefore **put to death** your members which are on the earth: fornication, uncleanness, passion, evil desire, and covetousness, which is idolatry. ⁶ Because of these things the wrath of God is coming upon the sons of disobedience, ⁷ in which you yourselves **once** walked when you lived in them.*

Of course, you know the little expression, "When you see the word 'therefore', find out what it's there for". So, let's take a look at the verses right before the above passage.

Colossians 3:1-4

*If then **you were raised** with Christ, seek those things which are above, where Christ is, sitting at the right hand of God. ² Set your mind on things above, not on things on the earth. ³ **For you died**, and your life is hidden with Christ in God. ⁴ When Christ **who is our life** appears, then you also will appear with Him in glory. ⁵ **Therefore** (because you already died with Christ) put to death...*

Paul is not telling the Colossians to die. He's telling them that *because* they already died and rose with Christ, they were to now put to death sin in their lives. I see us as warriors with total authority vanquishing our foes. We stand victorious and overcome any temptation we might face. Here's a parallel verse.

Romans 6:11-14

*Likewise you also, reckon yourselves to be **dead indeed to sin**, but **alive** to God in Christ Jesus our Lord. ¹² **Therefore** (because you were already crucified with Him and are now alive to God and free from sin) do not let sin reign in your mortal body, that you should obey it in its lusts. ¹³ And do not present your members as instruments of unrighteousness to sin, but present yourselves to God **as being alive from the dead**, and your members as instruments of righteousness to God. ¹⁴ For sin shall not have dominion over you, for you are not under law but under grace.*

The sinners we *were*, died, and now we live as the righteous. Because of this we now have the authority to refuse to allow sin to rule us. This is His doing, and we simply walk in it.

So, what did Jesus mean when He told those following Him to pick up their cross and follow Him? It would seem on the surface that this would negate what I have just shown.

Luke 9:20-26

*He said to them, "But who do you say that I am?" Peter answered and said, "The Christ of God." *[21]* And He strictly warned and commanded them to tell this to no one, *[22]* saying, "**The Son of Man must suffer many things, and be rejected by the elders and chief priests and scribes, and be killed, and be raised the third day.**" *[23]* Then He said to them all, "If anyone desires to come after Me, let him deny himself, and take up his cross (daily), and follow Me. *[24]* For whoever desires to save his life will lose it, but whoever loses his life for My sake will save it. *[25]* For what profit is it to a man **if he gains the whole world, and is himself destroyed or lost**? *[26]* For whoever is ashamed of Me and My words, of him the Son of Man will be ashamed when He comes in His own glory, and in His Father's, and of the holy angels.*

Jesus was speaking of His own upcoming death when He told them to take up their cross and follow Him. We know that they were not at that time going to be physically crucified with Jesus and that instead of picking up their crosses, they fled in fear; so of course, He was referring to the fact that they would soon be "crucified with Christ" just as Paul would later declare that he had been crucified (Gal. 2:20). The "whoever" of whom Jesus is speaking in this passage are those who have not yet been born again (no one had at this time). If someone refuses to die with Christ, he will end up losing his life. If we die with Him, we will live. If someone is ashamed to confess Jesus as the Lord, that person will be lost.

That's easy enough to show, but then why does Jesus tell them to pick their cross "daily"? There are only two possible answers based on what we have already seen (that believers already died). The first would be that just as Paul "died daily" through the hardships and persecutions he suffered for Christ, so will all believers who follow Jesus die "daily" by not being ashamed of Him and His words, and of course, it is true that we will all suffer persecution. So, this explanation makes sense, but I think it is also significant to consider that the exact same accounts in both Mark 8:34 and Matthew 26:24 do not include the word "daily". The possible addition of this one word in Luke 9:23, seems to change the whole meaning of the passage from a one-time death to a series of deaths. Interestingly enough, according to the Nelson NKJV study Bible, the word "daily" does not appear in the Greek New Testament According to the Majority Text. This, along with the fact that no New Testament writer instructs the believers to die, let alone to die daily, leads us to a fair speculation that the word "daily" might have been added later by a well-meaning translator.

This possible explanation aside, it still remains that we *were* crucified with Jesus and buried with Him in baptism. I believe this is what Jesus meant when He said to pick up our cross—that those who followed Him would be crucified with Him once and for all time, just as Jesus only died one time and was once buried. Yet we are no longer dead. We were raised with Him and now we live.

Life! Everlasting life! It seems to me that this is something that is almost never talked about in church; certainly not as much as "dying", but life—*everlasting* **life** is what Jesus died and rose again to give us! When we begin to focus on what Jesus died to give us, we begin to see that living in this everlasting life, not dying, is the point.

John 3:16
For God so **LOVED** *the world that He* **GAVE** *His only begotten Son, that whoever believes in Him should not perish but have* **everlasting LIFE**.

John 4:14
*"Whoever drinks of the water that I shall give him will never thirst. But the water that I shall give him will become in him a fountain of water springing up into **everlasting LIFE**."*

John 10:10
*The thief does not come except to steal, and to kill, and to destroy. I have come that they may have **LIFE**, and that they may have it more **abundantly**.*

Titus 3:4-7
*But when the kindness and the love of God our Savior toward man appeared, ⁵ not by works of righteousness which we have done, but according to His mercy He saved us, through the washing of regeneration and renewing of the Holy Spirit, ⁶ whom He poured out on us abundantly through Jesus Christ our Savior, ⁷ that having been justified by His grace we should become heirs according to the **hope of eternal LIFE**.*

1 John 5:11-13
*And the testimony is this, that God **has given** us **eternal LIFE**, and this **LIFE** is in **His Son**. ¹² He who has the Son has the **LIFE**; he who does not have the Son of God does not have the life. ¹³ These things I have written to you who believe in the name of the Son of God, so that you may **know** that you have **eternal LIFE**.*

The gospel, the good news, is that Jesus didn't come to give us eternal death. He came to give us eternal life! This life has been *given* to us by grace through faith. So, let us celebrate and proclaim life! In doing so, we will be preaching the true gospel.

Day 26

IN THE SPIRIT OR IN THE FLESH

*A*re believers "in the Spirit" or are we "in the flesh"? There are two big hurdles to face when attempting to answer this question. One difficulty we confront comes from the multiple uses of the word "flesh" (sarx) in Scripture which vary in meaning based on context. Generally speaking, "flesh" can refer to actual flesh (Lk. 24:39, Jn. 6:51), kindred relationships (Rom. 9:3), the state of being human (Gal. 1:16, Gal. 2:20, Eph. 6:12), personal abilities or religious accomplishments (Phil. 3:3-4, Gal. 3:3), human desires (Rom 13:14), the "flesh" as opposed to the spiritual (Mt. 16:17, Jn. 1:13, Jn. 6:63), and our condition before coming to faith in Christ (Rom. 7:5, Gal. 5:24, Eph.2:3, Jn. 3:6, Rom. 8:9). If we are unaware of these different uses, we can become confused as to who we are in Him when we read the word "flesh". We are "flesh" in the sense of being human, for example, and this life we are now living we live "in the flesh", in the sense of "in this body". **These have to do with our current mortal state, and not our standing before God in Christ.** Here is a classic example. When Paul writes "in the flesh" in this verse, he is not declaring anything negative about himself. He is referring to the life he lived in his human body.

205

Galatians 2:20
I have been crucified with Christ; it is no longer I who live, but Christ lives in me; and the life which I now live in the flesh I live by faith in the Son of God, who loved me and gave Himself for me.

The other obstacle we face, perhaps more formidable, is tradition. Now, tradition, in and of itself, is not evil, if that tradition is based on truth. However, when our traditions are not founded on truth, we can become confused and irrational in our thinking.

David's and my former understanding of this topic was based on tradition, one that is still believed by many Christians today. We believed that Christians have a choice of whether to be in the Spirit or in the flesh. We viewed "being in the Spirit" as choosing to do what is right and dedicating ourselves to spiritual disciplines such as prayer and Bible reading. "Being in the flesh" we saw as giving into our fleshly desires and neglecting spiritual practices. We never stopped to analyze what we were actually thinking—that we believed that we were "in the Spirit" based on following laws and by our own religious effort instead of on what Jesus accomplished in us.

Let us consider these very crucial passages to further our understanding.

Jesus, in speaking of being born again, said, "That which is born of the flesh is flesh, and that which is born of the Spirit **is spirit**," (Jn. 3:6). Since we Christians are born of the Spirit, then we are spirit, correct?

Paul wrote, "And those who belong to Christ Jesus **have crucified** the flesh with its passions and desires. Since we live **by the Spirit**, let us also be guided by the Spirit," (Gal. 5:24-25 MOUNCE). So, we who belong to Christ Jesus have crucified the flesh, right? We believers live by the Spirit, don't we?

Paul also declared, "But you are **not in the flesh but in the Spirit**, if indeed the Spirit of God dwells in you. Now if anyone does not have the Spirit of Christ He is not His,"

(Rom. 8:9). Does the Spirit of God dwell in believers? Do we have the Spirit of Christ? Are we His? Yes, yes, and yes indeed! So, then, we are in the Spirit and not in the flesh, are we not?

It is from this perspective that we can answer the question emphatically. **Believers are in the Spirit at all times.** "Being in the Spirit" isn't based on what we *do*, but on the Person in whom we have *believed.* Because we believe in Him, because we are born again, we are spirit not flesh. When we understand this, we see that Romans 8:1-17 is not as a discussion of *believers* being sometimes in the Spirit and sometimes in the flesh (which is what we used to believe until only four years ago), but it is a demonstration of the differences between those who are in the flesh, non-believers, and those who are in the Spirit, believers.

> [1] *There is therefore now no condemnation **to those who are in Christ Jesus**, who do not walk according to the flesh, but according to the Spirit.*[65]

Now, formerly we interpreted this to mean, that if we would walk according to the Spirit and not according to the flesh, there would be no condemnation for us. However, now with the understanding that believers *are* in the Spirit, this verse lights up. Those who are in Christ Jesus are those who do not walk according to the flesh, but according to the Spirit—we believers. For us, there is no condemnation.

> [2] *For the law of the Spirit of life in Christ Jesus has made me free from the law of sin and death.* [3] *For what the law could not do in that it was weak through the flesh, God did by sending His own Son in the likeness of sinful flesh, on account of sin: He condemned sin in the flesh,* [4] *that the **righteous***

---

[65] Some excellent translations omit the second half of verse 1. I won't debate that here.

requirement of the law *might be fulfilled in* **us who do not walk according to the flesh but according to the Spirit.**

We walk in the Spirit because we are free from the law.[66] The law could not make us perfect, but Jesus fulfilled the righteous requirement of the law in those who do not walk according to the flesh but according to the Spirit—in other words, in believers.

> *⁵ For those who live according to the flesh set their minds on the things of the flesh, but those who live according to the Spirit, the things of the Spirit.*

Paul is saying that non-believers, those who are in the flesh, set their minds on the things of the flesh, but we, believers, set our minds on the things of the Spirit. We could not do this if Jesus had not made us new creations. It is now our divine nature to focus on the Spirit and not the flesh.

> *⁶ For to be carnally minded is death, but to be spiritually minded is life and peace. ⁷ Because the carnal mind is enmity against God; for it is not subject to the law of God, nor indeed can be. ⁸ So then, those who are in the flesh cannot please God.*

Too long we have used this verse to tell believers that they are not pleasing God if they are "carnally minded", but Paul is not saying that. He is showing a contrast between the righteous and sinners. *Sinners* are carnally minded. Their minds are opposed to God and not subject to the law of God. In fact, Paul says, as if to make it entirely clear, they *cannot* be subject to the law of God, which he would have never said about believers. Those who are in

---

[66] The correlation between the law and the flesh is greater than we ever understood.

the flesh—sinners, as opposed to those who are in the Spirit—believers, cannot please God. However, those who are in the Spirit—we believers, do please God. Now, Paul clarifies.

*⁹ But **you** are **not** in the flesh but in the Spirit, if indeed the Spirit of God dwells in you. Now if anyone does not have the Spirit of Christ, he is not His.*

What is the qualification that Paul gives to be in the Spirit—isn't it that the Spirit of God dwells in us? The Spirit of God permanently dwells in believers (Jn. 14:16). Thus, we are in the Spirit and we are His.

¹⁰ And if Christ is in you, the body is dead because of sin, but the Spirit is life because of righteousness.

Christ is in us, and we are dead to sin as Paul just penned in Romans 6, but the Spirit is life because we have been made righteous. We are no longer dead sinners under law and dominated by flesh. We are the living righteous under grace and freed from sin.

¹¹ But if the Spirit of Him who raised Jesus from the dead dwells in you, He who raised Christ from the dead will also give life to your mortal bodies through His Spirit who dwells in you.

This is our present and future hope. God, who raised Jesus from the dead, dwells in us, and He will raise our mortal bodies by His Spirit. This mortal will put on immortality.

¹² Therefore, brethren, we are debtors—not to the flesh, to live according to the flesh. ¹³ For if you live according to the flesh you will die; but if by the Spirit you put to death the deeds of the body, you will live.

Most translations of these verses lean toward the understanding that if *believers* live according to the flesh, they will die, and if they live according to the Spirit, they will live. Think about this, please. Is our eternal salvation to be determined this way? Are we saved initially by grace through faith (not of works), but then after salvation life or death is determined by whether we live according to the Spirit or the flesh? Now, perhaps it would be reasonable to say that wrong choices keep us from enjoying the life we've been given, but these verses aren't normally taught this way.

The only way we can make sense of these verses is to recognize that Paul is continuing to contrast the believer and the non-believer. Those who are in the Spirit, believers, are not obligated to the flesh. We are the ones who put to death the deeds of the body and have life. Those who live according to the flesh, non-believers, are headed toward death.

Notice that the next verse affirms this truth: that the sons of God are led by the Spirit of God (not the flesh).

¹⁴ For as many as are led (who are being constantly led)[67] by the Spirit of God, these are sons of God.

Verse fourteen is not saying that we need to *try* to be led by the Spirit of God (as I thought for most of my Christian life), nor is it saying that we are led by the Spirit of God *if* we are in the Spirit not the flesh (since believers *are* in the Spirit). It is saying that since we are the sons of God, we *are* being led by the Spirit of God. What a different perspective. It takes all the work and mystery out of this whole idea of being led by the Spirit. He leads. We

---

[67] Wuest Expanded Translation

follow. How simple and revolutionary. What rest! We are in the Spirit and we can trust that He is leading.

Let us also look at a somewhat parallel passage in Galatians 5:16-18

> *I say then: Walk in the Spirit, and you shall not fulfill the lust of the flesh. ¹⁷ For the flesh lusts against the Spirit, and the Spirit against the flesh; and these are contrary to one another, so that you do not do the things that you wish. ¹⁸ **But if you are led by the Spirit, you are not under the law.***

Remember that Galatians is Paul's rebuke for those who were adding law to grace, who began "in the Spirit" but then were trying to be perfected by the flesh—by obeying laws. Notice in verse 18, Paul shows that those who are led by the Spirit, which we now know means the sons of God, are not under law. When we try to add law to grace we end up like Paul in Romans 7, not doing the things we wish to do and doing the things we don't want to do. This is important to connect with "fulfilling the lust of the flesh". **The flesh is closely associated with law.** We are not under the law. We are not in the flesh. We are under grace. We are in the Spirit. So, because we are not in the flesh, but in the Spirit, we simply walk in the Spirit—in grace not law.

Romans 6:14 Amplified
For sin shall not [any longer] exert dominion over you, since now you are not under Law [as slaves], but under grace [as subjects of God's favor and mercy].

I hope you are beginning to see this glorious truth. We are new creations who are in the Spirit not the flesh. It is our new nature to love God and want to please Him. We don't need to be led by the law because we *are* led by the Spirit. Glory to God in the highest!

Day 27

TO SERVE OR BE SERVED

---

*O*ne afternoon after a particularly demanding period of time, I stopped what I was doing to pray because I was feeling the demands of ministry beginning to overwhelm me. Now, I need to explain that my husband works full-time in a "secular" job and works in the ministry in his "spare" time. He travels a lot during the day and is constantly coming and going. On top of that he is very diligent to share in the responsibilities of our home, and he pampers me beyond belief! Since I work from home, I have more time to work on ministry details. This means that I do most of the administration, communications, merging of our study notes into outlines, reproduction of teaching materials, mailings, and PowerPoint presentations for both our lessons and music. I should also note that I *love* doing these things and recognize that He has given me the grace of administration.

It was a particularly stressful season for me since the holidays were just winding down and a new year was beginning. David, much to my delight, got an organizing "bug" and was busy emptying every file and drawer that pertained to him and filing, shredding, and putting this and that "in its place". I was in the background working on ministry responsibilities and beginning to notice that his busy schedule and organizing was causing him to get back-logged on our normal preparations which meant I was involuntarily getting behind. This started to weigh on me, and I admit I was beginning to feel a *tad* resentful.

"Lord, tell David to help me!" I prayed, not believing the words that just came out of my mouth, shaking my head and chuckling at myself before the Lord as I prayed.

Luke 10:38-40
Now it happened as they went that He entered a certain village; and a certain woman named Martha welcomed Him into her house. ³⁹ And she had a sister called Mary, who also sat at Jesus' feet and heard His word. ⁴⁰ But Martha was distracted with much serving, and she approached Him and said, **"Lord, do You not care that my sister has left me to serve alone? Therefore tell her to help me."**

Now, most Christians are aware of this passage and its import, but how many of us who work in ministry have prayed, "Lord, give me more Marthas!" or "Lord, tell them to help me,"?

It's so easy to take potshots at ministers, and honestly, I get tired of hearing all the pastor bashing that goes on in social media—viewing them *all* as greedy for gain and power. I'm not saying this does not exist. It does; but before you begin to hurl insults and accusations, please consider the demands on the modern-day pastor.

Most people don't realize how much work it is to oversee a ministry. The Christian public has certain expectations today about finding what we call a "full-service" church, one that offers not only a dynamic Sunday morning service replete with a sermon that will minister to everyone in attendance (nowadays with aspects of a multi-media presentation) and a professionally polished worship service, but also an exciting children's ministry, a meaningful, involved, and vibrant youth group, an aesthetically pleasing and meticulously clean facility, friendly greeters, a much-needed nursery, an office staff that is kind and helpful during the week, benevolence services for those in need, marriages, funerals, small groups, evangelism, outreach into the community, hospital and prison visitation, the righting of injustices, an awesome website replete with the latest multi-media, and to top it all off, a school from preschool through high school, etc., etc., etc. Obviously, no pastor and his wife can do all of these things themselves. It takes "everyone" working together to develop a gathering place with these services.[68]

Most of us in ministry have been in more than one "leadership" meeting where someone complains that 20% of the people are doing 80% of the work, and that someone should encourage the people of the church to "come and help" them. That "someone", of course, is the pastor. Oh, and please add that to the list of things the pastor is supposed to do—motivate people to serve!

So, without giving consideration to the fact that the complaint is identical to Martha's, the much needed teaching series begins, usually in the form of "helping" people to find their gifts in the body of Christ. This series is usually concluded by giving opportunities for individual service within that local assembly. This is not to say that "equipping the saints for the work of the ministry" is inappropriate, but that it is often motivated by the need for more workers. What we are really doing is recruiting and developing Marthas.

Even though we know the story, we still persist in this madness referring to those who are not involved in the ministry of the church as mere "pew warmers". These pew-warming Marys drop off their children in the nursery and Sunday School, and walk in the sanctuary door. They seem so happy to see all the Marthas again as they scurry about "serving the Lord" while these lazy Marys have the nerve to just sit there receiving the word—not lifting one finger to help! They get to go home and spend the rest of the day with

---

[68] I realize that many of my contemporaries in the gospel of grace renewal will dispute whether this form of gathering is even Scriptural. I do not wish to debate that here. I am speaking of the realities of our current perception of "church" and its cultural context.

their families while the Marthas clean-up and get ready for another Sunday ministry.

"Lord, tell them to help me!"

Luke 10:41-42
*And Jesus answered and said to her, "Martha, Martha, you are worried and troubled about many things. ⁴² But **one thing** is needed, and Mary has chosen that good part, which will not be taken away from her."*

What was that "good part" which would not be taken from Mary? It only says that she "sat at Jesus' feet and heard His word". Many traditionally have seen this as a call to prayer (sitting at Jesus feet) and reading the Bible each day (hearing His word).

Now, here's where it gets a little complicated. Most Marthas, and I'd say "especially" Marthas in the church today, already have a consistent prayer life and read the Bible nearly daily, and some of them do this for the express purpose of being a Mary. Then, they get up and think and behave as did Martha, faithfully "serving the Lord" while sometimes resenting that they have been left to do all the work alone.

Was Jesus really giving a lesson on the importance of prayer and Bible study? We should be significantly struck by Jesus saying that "one" thing was needful. If what Jesus meant to teach was that we need to have prayer *and* Bible study, why didn't He say "two" things? Think about this for a minute. What really is that "one" thing if not these two things?

Picture the scene. Jesus came to Martha's house. The long-awaited Messiah just walked into her home. The Messiah, mind you! Mary did the right thing and took a seat as close as she could so she could hear His word. Martha did the polite thing and began to prepare a meal.

What was the word that Jesus spoke to Mary? What was the word the Messiah preached? Was it not the good news of the kingdom of God?

215

I believe that the one thing Mary chose was to hear Jesus. We don't know his exact words to Mary but we can assume that just as Jesus did everywhere (Mk. 2:2), He was sharing the gospel. Maybe He told those listening along with Mary a parable or talked about being born again or perhaps one of His other messages. The point is, Jesus came to Martha and Mary's house not so that Mary and Martha would serve *Him* a luscious meal, but with the purpose of serving *them* the good news.

Did Jesus say, "Come unto me all you who are weary and heavy-laden, and I will put you to work serving me"?

Matthew 11:28-29

Come to Me, all you who labor and are heavy laden, and I will **give** *you* **rest**. *29 Take My yoke upon you and* **learn from Me**, *for I am gentle and lowly in heart, and you will find* **rest** *for your souls. 30 For My yoke is* **easy** *and My burden is* **light**.*"*

The pressure to perform is tremendous in most churches, particularly upon the pastor (and his family). Knowing he can't possibly do it all, he then delegates responsibilities to those who are willing to help him. Soon, there can be a whole ministry staff stressed out beyond their own belief. Then after all this hard work takes effect (*if* it takes effect) and the church begins to grow, the need for more Marthas seems to grow exponentially.

Where is the "one" thing? Where is the good news? So many of us are weary or in need of healing. Instead of hearing that Jesus is our Healer and that He is reaching out to *us* in love, we are inspired to work harder for the Lord to prove *our* love. Many believers today are held captive, some of them by their excessive compulsion to serve, others by sin they never imagined would plague them. Will we teach them the truth that sets free or continue to condemn for weakness? Many more are blind. Shouldn't we teach them the truth that will open their eyes instead of heaping on burdens that we cannot possibly bear? And what about the oppressed; those who are heavy laden by laws and traditions that increase each week? They need to know that Jesus came to serve them, to love them, to give them freedom. Where is the gospel, the good news about what Jesus did and who He made us? **With most viewing the gospel as something for the lost, the good news is seldom taught to the saved.** Without this one thing, without hearing the glad tidings of good things from our benevolent God, the focus is turned upon the ministry instead of on Him. **When our focus becomes serving *Him*, instead of what He has done to serve *us*, we quickly become Marthas.** Please read that sentence again.

What is the answer to this puzzle? Grace, of course!

1 Corinthians 15:10
*But by the **grace** of God I am what I am, and His **grace** toward me was not in vain; but I labored more abundantly than they all, yet not I, but the **grace** of God which was with me.*

We know how diligently Paul worked. Most of his ministry, he supported himself financially (and those with him) by working as a tent maker. This, no doubt, took many hours a day. Yet he and his fellow-workers turned much of the then known world upside down! How did they do this? By His abundant grace.

When we preach the gospel of God's unmeritted favor and love for His people, something happens that is far superior to our efforts to train Marthas. When believers are fed with the good news of what *Jesus* did and does to serve and love *us* the rivers of living water begin to flow and all the fruit of the Spirit begins to grow. When we, like Mary, "hear His word", the gospel, and allow Jesus to serve us, when we receive from Him all the good He has done for us and all the good He is still giving us; the good works for which we were created, simply happen.

Jesus made a very interesting statement.

Matthew 20:24-28

*And when the ten heard it, they were greatly displeased with the two brothers. ²⁵ But Jesus called them to Himself and said, "You know that the rulers of the Gentiles lord it over them, and those who are great exercise authority over them. ²⁶ Yet it shall not be so among you; but whoever desires to become great among you, let him be your servant. ²⁷ And whoever desires to be first among you, let him be your slave— ²⁸ just as the Son of Man **did not come to be served, but to serve**, and to give His life a ransom for many."*

Jesus did not come to be served, but to serve, and to give His life a ransom *for us*. So, we automatically jump into "follow Jesus' example" mode and overlook the impact of what Jesus is saying. We cannot skip this first step: Jesus came to **serve** *us*. He has done so much for us that we can spend our lifetimes discovering it all. He continues to serve us throughout our lives. His heart is all about serving us, not us serving Him. This goes against *everything* my husband and I believed and all that we practiced. **Jesus did *not* come to be served, but to serve.**

So, the first step is to let Jesus serve us.

"Martha, thank-you for all the work you are doing to make my visit a pleasant one, but I did not come to your house today so that you would serve *Me*. I came to serve *you*. Please come and sit here with your sister and hear the good news of the Father's great love for you."

Many in the church today think that people who preach grace as God's unmerited favor are presenting some sort of candy man God, always giving out prizes. We tend to find it selfish to think that any one of us would focus on what *God* gives *us* instead of what *we* can give *Him*. Yet, Jesus is the one who said that He did not come to be served, but to serve. He was the one who **commended Mary for *receiving* from Him**.

So—Jesus serves us, then we serve Him, right? No, not exactly. Look again at verses 26 and 27. Jesus serves us, and then we serve each other.

We get our heads screwed on backwards. We see being involved in church ministries and all of our other spiritual disciplines as "serving the Lord", but what we should do is let Him first serve us, then labor to serve and love *each other* as He commanded.

Jesus said, "These things I have spoken to you, that My joy may remain in you, and that your joy may be full. [12] This is My commandment, that you love one another as I have loved you. [13] Greater love has no one than this, than to lay down one's life for his friends. [14] You are My friends if you do whatever I command you (Jn. 15:11-14).

Jesus loved us. He gave His life for us. Now, he wants us to love and serve each other. What is His motivation? "That your joy may be full and that My joy may remain in you."

That "one thing" that Mary chose was hearing the word of Jesus which was the gospel of His grace. In doing so, she knew she was loved. He was giving to her and she was receiving from Him. He was serving her while Martha was focusing on serving Him. This is the most important thing for every Christian—to take time to hear His glad tidings of good things, of the love that caused Him to give His life for us. When we deeply know His love, serving each other is a joy, and He receives that service toward each other as love unto Himself.

Matthew 25:37-40

*"Then the righteous will answer Him, saying, 'Lord, when did we see You hungry and feed You, or thirsty and give You drink? [38] When did we see You a stranger and take You in, or naked and clothe You? [39] Or when did we see You sick, or in prison, and come to You?' [40] And the King will answer and say to them, 'Assuredly, I say to you, **inasmuch as you did it to one of the least of these My brethren, you did it to Me.**'"*

Let's allow Jesus to serve and love us by teaching us the glad tidings of good things from our benevolent God. Then and only then can we effectively serve and love each other. How and when this love and service from God comes is not important—only that we allow it. We need to make His love for us be the focus of our study. When we are in need, we simply remember His love and let Him serve us. What we are doing is just letting the rivers of living water flow into us and then we are equipped to let them flow out of us.

When we serve and love each other, then we are serving and loving God. What a beautiful circle of love and grace! He loves and serves us. We receive His love and service to us. We love and serve each other. He receives our love and service for each other as love and service toward Him.

Might the church as we know it fall apart without more Marthas? This is a reasonable question, and I think the logical answer is, "It might." At the very least the church will change considerably. Would this be so awful? Wouldn't it be a good thing if all of us simply received from Jesus? Then wouldn't letting people minister to each other, instead of feeling "the church" must minister to each and every aspect of someone's life not be a healthy step?

I believe as we learn more about the true gospel, we will see drastic changes in our church structures and ministries, but this need not be a negative thing, but one which will bring relief and rest to those who are weary. We must keep in mind that our focus is not to be on building a full-service organized church or building a ministry for ourselves, but on serving the sheep the pure gospel. Feed and care for the sheep and they will grow, and God will be pleased, whether that is to 30 people or 30,000. It isn't the format that matters. It's the message. Focus on Jesus. Let Him serve you. Then serve each other. That's true ministry.

Day 28

COMMON CONCERNS

*D*uring the time David and I have been sharing the gospel of the grace of God with fellow believers, we have discovered that even when we do our best to present it clearly, there are misunderstandings and genuine concerns that arise. The true gospel of grace is so radical, so extreme, that it can easily be mistaken for something it was never intended to be; precisely, a rationalization for continued sin or a reason for unjustifiable idleness. So, allow me to reiterate before the final chapters by answering some of the questions we've encountered over the years.

Q: Are you saying we should tear the Bible in half and throw the Old Testament into the trash?
A: Of course not! All Scripture is given by God's inspiration and is valuable to us today. However, it must be considered in its context and in light of the New Covenant. That is to say, all Scripture must be studied from the perspective of the cross of Christ.

John 5:39
You search the Scriptures, for in them you think you have eternal life; and these are they which testify of Me.

Q: Shouldn't grace be balanced with truth, law, works, and obedience?

A: No! The very nature of God's grace is that it is unbalanced—in our favor. It can't be earned by our works. It can't be maintained by following laws. It can't be improved by obedience. Jesus Christ is the way, the truth, and the life. He is God's grace demonstrated to us. How we live after we receive this grace is a fruit of what He has done.

> ### John 1:16-17
> *And of His fullness we have all received, and grace for grace.[17] For the law was given through Moses, but grace and truth came through Jesus Christ.*

Q: Are you saying that we don't have to obey God?

A: I'm saying that born again believers WANT to obey. Our first obedience is to the faith; that is, to believe in Jesus. After that God works in us "to will and to do His good pleasure".

Q: Don't we have to cooperate with God in order to stay in His grace?

A: If cooperation is required to "stay" in His grace then that would make His grace something that we must earn or maintain, and it would thus be merited and no longer be grace. We are righteous by grace through faith as a gift, and that righteousness before God is a settled fact due to Christ's sacrifice for us. We are new creations with new natures that *want* to please God. I don't *have* to please God. I *want* to please Him. That's the core difference between law and grace. Law requires. Grace sets free.

Q: What about willful disobedience?

A: The willful disobedience spoken of in Hebrews is referring to apostasy[69] (Heb. 10:26-39); not as we commonly

---

[69] Others argue that willful disobedience is the sin of rejecting Jesus as a non-believer. Either way one views it, "willful disobedience" is not referring to a deliberate sin since most sin is intentional.

teach, that of committing a sin on purpose. The truth is, all the sins we commit are on purpose; otherwise, that would mean that we have no control over our actions. If willful sin, as we commonly teach it to be, brings about a state in which the person cannot be saved, then there will be no one in heaven.

Q: Are you saying that we only have to *believe* to be righteous before God?
A: Yes, all we have to do is believe in the resurrection and confess Jesus as the Lord to be born again and receive all that He died to give us. We do not do good works to better our right-standing before God because *righteousness is a gift*. Our faith in His grace will bring about the good works for which God has ordained us.

Ephesians 2:8-10
For by grace you have been saved through faith, and that not of yourselves; it is the gift of God, ⁹ not of works, lest anyone should boast. ¹⁰ For we are His workmanship, created in Christ Jesus for good works, which God prepared beforehand that we should walk in them.

Roman 5:17-21
*For if by the one man's offense death reigned through the one, much more those who receive abundance of grace and of the **gift of righteousness** will reign in life through the One, Jesus Christ. ¹⁸ Therefore, as through one man's offense judgment came to all men, resulting in condemnation, even so through one Man's righteous act the free gift came to all men, resulting in justification of life. ¹⁹ **For as by one man's disobedience many were made sinners, so also by one Man's obedience many will be made righteous.** ²⁰ Moreover the law entered that the offense might abound. **But where sin abounded, grace abounded much more, ²¹ so that as sin reigned in death, even so grace***

might reign through righteousness to eternal life through Jesus Christ our Lord.

Q: Then, what about what James said about being justified by our works?
A: If James meant that works are required for right-standing with God, then he was preaching "another" gospel and is accursed. Since we don't believe this is the case, the only logical conclusion that can be made is that in the context given, James meant that faith will bring about good works. If there are no good works, it is likely that the individual is not truly born again (does not have faith in Jesus—his faith is dead) or that he is living under law which has caused him to sin.

> *Matthew 7:15-20*
> *"Beware of false prophets, who come to you in sheep's clothing, but inwardly they are ravenous wolves.* *[16] You will know them by their fruits. Do men gather grapes from thorn bushes or figs from thistles?* *[17] Even so, **every good tree bears good fruit,** but a bad tree bears bad fruit.* *[18] A good tree cannot bear bad fruit, nor can a bad tree bear good fruit.* *[19] Every tree that does not bear good fruit is cut down and thrown into the fire.* *[20] Therefore **by their fruits you will know them.***

Q: Are you saying that sin is no big deal?
A: God forbid! Sin is why Jesus died for us—to save us from our sin. God's desire for us is to be truly free from sin. However, God is no longer imputing our sin to us, and He is remembering our lawless deeds no more. God's desire is for us not to sin, but if we sin, we are forgiven. Furthermore, it isn't adherence to law that sets us free from sin. It is God's grace.

1 John 2:1
*My little children, these things I write to you, so that you may **not sin**. And if anyone sins, we have an Advocate with the Father, Jesus Christ the righteous.*
Romans 6:14
*For sin shall **not** have dominion over you, for you are **not** under law but under **grace**.*

Q: Do you believe that a true believer in Jesus who is involved in sin is still saved?
A: Yes. Sin was forgiven at the cross and God is no longer holding our sins against us (2 Cor. 5:19). When we sin, His blood is already cleansing us (1 Jn. 1:7). The only sin for which man will be lost is that of refusing to believe in Jesus Christ (Jn. 3:18). However, if someone is truly born again, they will not want to sin, unless they have come back under law in some way, which strengthens sin (1 Cor. 15:56). This person's only hope is to come back under grace and forsake law.

Q: You say that believers are not sinners. Isn't that a form of elitism?
A: I believe Romans 6 makes it very clear that believers are dead to and free from sin. Since this is true of *all* believers and not just some special class of overcomers, it isn't elitism.

Q: What about church discipline? Are you saying we just let people "live like the devil" while touting grace?
A: No. There are situations where it is necessary to address individual destructive behavior, especially when it affects the lives of others. There are also laws in most states which make ministers mandatory reporters for suspected child abuse. It would be wrong to shelter a child abuser in the name of grace, for example, since his behavior is criminal.

However, we need to take a closer look at how Paul addressed church discipline. He did not use law or the threat of eternal damnation or the fear of missing the rapture to correct poor behavior. He first taught the people about who they were in Jesus and what He accomplished for them. Then he encouraged them to live correctly *because* of what they'd been given and who they were.

Since a born again person is no longer a sinner, but a righteous person, it is only logical that he should live in a way that reflects this righteousness. We are clearly instructed to not sin. However, there are many believers today overtaken by sin who are in this state because they have been fed a mixture of grace and law most of their Christian lives. This resulted in finding themselves in the hopeless state described in Romans 7 where they can't do the good they want nor stop doing the evil they are doing. We need to help them recognize that they are to be motivated and taught by grace so that they may live in Romans 6-8, free from sin, dead to the law, and led by the Spirit.

Q: Since we are continually cleansed from all sin, are you saying there will be no consequence for that sin?
A: There are clearly consequences for sin—sometimes horrific. For example, someone who drinks excessively and then drives might not only kill himself, but multiple others. Those engaging in sexual sins expose themselves to sexually transmitted diseases. A man who commits adultery might discover that his wife is not willing to stay married to him and lose at least partial custody of his children. Someone who continues in sin (ignoring the grace of God who is teaching him to forsake it) can experience a dulling of their conscience and become involved in other unhealthy behaviors. These are logical consequences for sin, not judgments doled out by God.

A Christian's sins are forgiven before God (1 Jn. 1:7). He is not casting down judgments for a Christian's weaknesses; rather, He is lovingly working in our lives all things for our good (Rom. 8:28). This is not to say He is indifferent about our sin or that He turns a blind eye; only that when we sin we have an Advocate with the Father who gave His only Son so that His blood would remove all sin from us forever (1 Jn. 2:1, Heb. 10:14). His Holy Spirit is constantly speaking to us

226

that we are children of God (Rom. 8:16). He is convincing us that we are righteous (Jn. 16:10).

His compassionate love will be there to help the erring believer to endure the pain that his sins might have caused. He will help him make the necessary restitution. If he is incarcerated, then Jesus will still be with Him in jail, and will work the awful situation for some good—perhaps to share God's love with others or to warn others to not "go there".

God will bring healing to the underserving one. For example, one of my dear friends who had liver disease from years of alcoholism was miraculous healed of it. Her life is now a testimony of God's power and grace. What we need to understand is that we are righteous by His grace through faith in His Son, not by never sinning. If refraining from sin is the standard for justification, we are all doomed, for even our every thought is in question; furthermore, Christ would not have needed to die for us if obedience to the law could bring righteousness.

Q: What about those who were obviously judged for sinning such as Ananias and Sapphira?
A: Receiving the truth about this account is difficult for those of us who were taught to believe that these people were Christians. We were warned that the same thing could happen to us if we weren't careful! However, a closer exam-ination of the text surrounding Ananais and Sapphira strongly suggests that they were not believers at all. They were mere imposters and mockers going through the motions in order to gain acceptance among the Christian community, likely for the benefits they perceived. They were the tares among the wheat that Jesus warned would be planted among us.

Matthew 13:24-30
Another parable He put forth to them, saying: "The kingdom of heaven is like a man who sowed good seed in his field; 25 but while men slept, his enemy came and sowed tares among the wheat and went his way. 26 But when the grain had sprouted and

227

produced a crop, then the tares also appeared. ²⁷ So *the servants of the owner came and said to him, 'Sir, did you not sow good seed in your field? How then does it have tares?' ²⁸ He said to them, 'An enemy has done this.' The servants said to him, 'Do you want us then to go and gather them up?' ²⁹ But he said, 'No, lest while you gather up the tares you also uproot the wheat with them. ³⁰ Let both grow together until the harvest, and at the time of harvest I will say to the reapers, "First gather together the tares and bind them in bundles to burn them, but gather the wheat into my barn.""*

When we look at the account of Ananias and Sapphira, we need to back up into chapter four where this type of giving was first described, and most closely the offering made by Barnabas. Now, we know without any doubt that Barnabas was a believer. However, notice that when the account shifts to Ananias and Sapphira, we see a contrast is being presented when Luke writes, "<u>But</u> a certain man named Ananias, with Sapphira his wife, sold a possession. ² And he kept back part of the proceeds, his wife also being aware of it, and brought a certain part and laid it at the apostles' feet." Nowhere does it state that they were believers, disciples, or brethren (the most common terms for Christians in the book of Acts),[70] but only as "a man and his wife".

Now let us apply the test of Matthew 7:15-20 as to the type of fruit apparent in the lives of Ananias and Sapphira. These two had no awareness that anyone would be able to perceive that they were lying—not even that God would notice! What believer, so recently born again would not be aware of God's omniscience? What believer would conspire to test God as they did? This pair seriously believed that they could pull this off, not just lie to the apostles, but to

---

[70] A very interesting study in the book of Acts is to read through it looking for the different names given to Christians. Overwhelmingly, it is clear in the context who was and who was not a believer.

God Himself! They had no consciousness that the Spirit of God even existed and had no fear lying to Him, even when confronted. This is strong evidence that they were not even Christians, but non-believers who were trying to blend in and obtain the status they thought such a gift would bring them.

Q: What about those who were sick and dying among the Corinthians? Weren't they judged with sickness and death for taking communion with unconfessed sin?
A: This passage has also been used to bring fear to the hearts of believers. We are often exhorted to confess any known sin and make sure no one has anything against us and that we have nothing against anyone before taking communion and we are warned that if we don't examine our-selves, we also might get sick or even die. Many believers today, out of fear that they might have some sin, refuse to take communion.

Yet, when Jesus first gave communion, he told His disciples to take the bread and the wine **in remembrance of *Him*** for as often as we do this we remember *His* death until He comes. He did not establish His table as a time to focus on *us* and *our* sin but as **a time to remember that His sacrifice *removed* our sins.** When we come to His table, we focus on the fact that His body was beaten and bruised for our healing and that the blood of Jesus cleanses us from *all* sin. **It is a time of remembrance and thankfulness, not a time for introspection.**

When Paul told them to examine themselves, I believe he meant to make sure they were in the faith. Imagine the scene Paul describes. Some came together to share in the Lord's table and had no reverence for God or understanding or appreciation of the beauty of the body and blood of the Lord whatsoever. They were using this gathering as a social event to eat and be drunk without even thinking to offer their plenty to the poor among them. Consider this behavior. Is this the fruit of the life of a believer? Jesus said that all men would know we are His disciples by our love for one another. These people were not showing love toward anyone but themselves. Paul admonishes them to discern the Lord's body, which apparently these were not doing. This is why I believe that those who were sick and dying among the Corinthians were non-believers who were in essence mocking the blood and body of the Lord and who had no regard for the brethren whom the Lord so deeply loves.

Jesus told us that we would be able to identify these imposters by their actions. Jude also gives an excellent description of these liars.

Jude 5, 12, 19-23
But I want to remind you, though you once knew this, that the Lord, having saved the people out of the land of Egypt, afterward destroyed those who did not believe (the context here is of non-believers)... *12 These are spots in your love feasts (love feasts included taking communion), while they feast with you **without fear**, serving only themselves. They are clouds without water, carried about by the winds; late autumn trees without fruit, twice dead, pulled up by the roots; 13 raging waves of the sea, foaming up their own shame; wandering stars for whom is reserved the blackness of darkness forever (clearly, this is a description of one who is devoid of the Spirit of God)...19 These are sensual persons, who cause divisions, not having the Spirit (now he makes it clear they do not have the Spirit and are thus not believers)...20 **But you** (referring to believers), **beloved**, building yourselves up on your most holy faith, praying in the Holy Spirit, 21 **keep yourselves in the love of God, looking for the mercy of our Lord Jesus Christ unto eternal life** (believers keep themselves in God's love and expect His mercy and eternal life). 22 And on some have compassion, **making a distinction** (the distinction is between believer and non-believer); 23 but others save with fear (the others are non-believers who need to be saved), pulling them out of the fire (non-believers*

*are destined for hell fire), hating even the garment
defiled by the flesh.*

**Q: If God judged Ananias and Sapphira and the
imposters in Corinth with sickness and death, why
aren't all sinners sick and dying?**
A: No one has ever asked us this question, but I believe
it should be asked and answered because something that
is seldom heard from the pulpit is that the sins of sinners
are forgiven or that God is not holding the sins of sinners
against them. Yet, we have two very amazing scriptures that
we must take into consideration.

1 John 2:1-2
*My little children, these things I write to you, so that
you may not sin. And if anyone sins, we have an
Advocate with the Father, Jesus Christ the righteous.*
*² And He Himself is the propitiation for our sins, and
not for ours only but also for the whole world.*
2 Corinthians 5:18-19
*Now all things are of God, who has reconciled us to
Himself through Jesus Christ, and has given us the
ministry of reconciliation, ¹⁹ that is, that God was in
Christ reconciling the world to Himself, **not imputing
their trespasses to them,** and has committed to us
the word of reconciliation.*

Sinners sin. That is a clear undeniable reality of which
God is fully aware. If God were killing off sinners for sinning
then all sinners would be dead. The truth is Jesus *died* for
sinners—all sinners. All of our sins were forgiven at the
cross. He is not holding our sins against us—none of us, not
even sinners!
However, and this is a big "however", apart from Christ,
all men stand guilty before God who refuse to believe in the
name of the Son of God.

John 3:18-19

He who believes in Him is not condemned; but he who does not believe is condemned already, **because he has not believed in the name of the only begotten Son of God.** *[19] And this is the condemnation, that the light has come into the world, and men loved darkness rather than light, because their deeds were evil.*

Sinners are condemned because they refuse to believe in the name of Jesus not because God is holding their sins against them. They refuse to believe because they love darkness instead of light. While forgiveness has been provided for them, they reject the source of that forgiveness.

Thus, faith in Jesus as the Lord God is the key to *receiving* the forgiveness that has already been provided, but if it is not received, those who reject Him will die in the very sins God is not holding against them. Jesus said, "Therefore I said to you that you will die in your sins; for **if you do not believe** that I am *He*, you will die in your sins," (Jn. 8:24).

As to the reconciling of sinners, as far as God is concerned, His work is done. Our message to sinners should be the good news, "God sent His Son to forgive you of your sins. He is not at war with you. He is extending to you reconciliation. Believe in Jesus and be reconciled to God." In other words, God is reconciled to man, **but man must reconcile himself to God through faith in Christ.**

2 Corinthians 5:20-21

Now then, we are ambassadors for Christ, as though God were pleading through us: we implore you on Christ's behalf, **be reconciled to God.** *[21] For He made Him who knew no sin to be sin for us, that we might become the righteousness of God in Him.*

As Christ's ambassadors, our message is, "Be reconciled to God. He became a sin offering for you so that you could become His very righteousness!"

232

I am NOT saying that everyone is already saved and that they just don't know it yet. That is heresy. I am saying that God has already died for the sins of the whole world and is already not holding the sins of sinners against them. His side of the equation was completed at the cross. However, salvation comes through confession of Jesus as the Lord God and belief in His resurrection. Period.

So, then, if this is the case, if God is not holding the sins of sinners against them, why were some judged with sickness and death? When we examine the instances of Ananias and Sapphira and those who were making a mockery of the Lord in Corinth, we see some remarkable similarities. (We should also include in this category the Sons of Sceva who attempted to cast out demons in the "name of Jesus whom Paul preaches".) First of all, they were imposters. They pretended to be part of the body of Christ, but were not. Two, they were not just sinning the sins that all sinners sin. They were brazenly and arrogantly testing the Holy Spirit. Ananias and Sapphira conspired together to put God to the test. Those in Corinth were making a mockery of the body and blood of the Lord. The Sons of Sceva dared use the name of Jesus to cast out demons for what could not have been anything but contemptuous motives. These stories were recorded, not to warn God's beloved children, but to warn anyone from without to be careful about similar fakery and mockery.

Q: Are you advocating "once saved always saved"?
A: This argument has been hotly debated throughout the centuries, and I have no illusions of ending the controversy here. David and I believe that we are saved by grace alone through faith in Jesus alone. Those who have faith in Jesus will not perish but have everlasting life and those who do not have faith in Jesus will perish (John 3:16-18). We do not believe sin will prevent a *believer* from going to heaven because all sin is forgiven and God is not imputing sin to us.

The crucial question really comes down to this, can a born again believer *forfeit* his salvation by choosing to abandon *faith* in Christ? Predictably, the grace camps are divided on this topic as were their forefathers. Some believe adamantly that it is *impossible* to forfeit salvation even if one appeared to forsake Christ since once we are born into the family, we remain in the family. Others believe that to forsake faith in Jesus is to commit apostasy and thus forsake salvation. A somewhat merged belief is that someone who is born again would never want to forsake faith in Christ, so then if someone did "forsake Christ" it would mean that the person was never born again in the first place. Each group has its own reasons and is usually convinced thoroughly of its conclusions.

Our belief is that faith in Jesus is what is required for salvation. Those who believe in Him will be saved. Those who don't, will not. There will be no one in heaven who does not believe in Jesus as the Lord.

Q: Do you believe that everyone will eventually be saved (universalism)?
A: No, faith in Jesus Christ is why we do not perish and have everlasting life (Jn. 3:16-18). Those who do not believe in Jesus are condemned for not believing and will perish.

Revelation 20:15
And anyone not found written in the Book of Life was cast into the lake of fire.

Q: If we don't teach the moral law, how will God's people know right from wrong?
A: God's grace will teach them as He writes His law of love on their hearts (Tit. 2:11-15).

Q: If we live under grace, not law, why does Paul give so many instructions about how we should live? Are these not New Covenant commandments for Christian living?
A: Paul, who so elegantly taught that we are not made righteous by following the law, did not then turn and give a new set of laws.

Too often we teach only on the chapters where Paul is giving correction. This correction, however, has a context. For example, in Ephesians, Paul writes three chapters declaring to the believers who they are in Christ and all the many things that are theirs in Christ. Then, after he has laid this foundation, he begins instructions on how these gifts affect our lives.

For example, a Sunday morning sermon might be Ephesians 4:1 which says, "I, therefore, the prisoner of the Lord, beseech you to walk worthy of the calling with which you were called." The sermon often continues on what it means to "walk worthy" and turns into what amounts to Christian laws, and this will be determined by what the teacher believes it means to "walk worthy".

However, Paul was not giving a set of commandments. He was saying, "In other words, because of what I have just shown you about who you are and the depths of God's love for you in Christ, walk in it!"

We, the church, usually skip the good news and jump directly into correction and instruction in righteousness. However, first we need to teach what God accomplished in Christ and of His endless love and grace toward us who believe. A Christian who knows he is loved and who allows God to love him will supernaturally want to live a holy life.

If this is so, then why does he have to say anything? Paul is completing the circle by showing our *response* to God's love. God gives generously. We receive in awe of His grace. His grace teaches us. We learn and live accordingly. Again, let me say, we do not live righteously in order to become righteous. We are righteous and therefore live righteously. It is our new supernatural nature to *want* to please God. Paul encourages believers to walk worthy of what they have been given which simply means to receive what we've been given and walk in it.

Q: If New Covenant believers taught by grace end up living in a way that looks like they are fulfilling the law, what's the difference if we teach law or grace? If the

outcome is the same, what's wrong with using laws to guide people?

A: The difference is crucial because Jesus fulfilled the law through His death (Gal. 3:13). Attempting to now be justified before God by following laws is to make His death a worthless act (Gal. 2:21). In Christ, we died to the law, our old husband, in order to be married to Christ (Rom. 7:1-6). To return to law for instruction instead of receiving guidance from grace is to commit spiritual adultery. Adding law to grace is like asking your former spouse to come and live with you and your new spouse, and then trying to please them both. The one who nags the most, the law, will win out eventually, and the new spouse, grace, will be nullified. Furthermore, teaching law actually strengthens sin (1 Cor. 15:56); whereas, grace frees us from the dominion of sin (Rom. 6:14). Finally, there is Paul's warning. Adding law to grace is to preach "another" gospel.

Q: Are you saying that Christians don't have to pray and read the Bible daily?

A: Yes, that is what I am saying. There is no law saying we *have* to pray and read the Bible as a daily discipline. There is no need to make prayer and Bible reading a *requirement* because a truly born again believer will *want* to pray and read the Bible. Both are a blessed irrevocable gift to us not a law. Sadly, many Christians today read the Bible and pray, not because they already have a close relationship with God but in order to obtain one. This monastic thinking is to try and accomplish through our own religious discipline what Jesus already purchased for us with His precious blood. **We do not get close or closer to God through prayer.** The blood of Jesus has brought us perfectly close. How can we improve upon what His blood accomplished? We pray *because* we have a close and right relationship with God not to get one.

1 Thessalonians 5:16-18
Rejoice always, ¹⁷ pray without ceasing, ¹⁸ in everything give thanks; for this is the will of God in Christ Jesus for you.

Q: Are you saying that it is WRONG to have a daily prayer time?
A. No, of course not. There is nothing wrong with setting aside a place and time to pray, as long as your time of prayer is *because* of your right-standing with God and not *in order to* obtain or maintain right-standing with God. **However, we must always keep in mind that this is a *personal* goal, not a God-given mandate, and God is not displeased or disappointed or angry with us if we don't keep the goals *we* set.** Also, it's important not to adapt heretical thinking which amounts to the idea that by praying more (your own effort) you will be *closer* to God or *more holy* or *more anointed.* Let me repeat this because it is so very important to understand. Prayer doesn't make you close or holy. The blood of Jesus accomplished this.

Q: Are you saying that you don't believe in progressive sanctification?
A: We are sanctified (made holy) by the one-time sacrifice of Jesus (Heb. 10:10) at salvation, AND Paul also spoke of being "sanctified completely" subsequent to salvation (1 Thess. 5:23-24). We are commanded to "be holy for I am holy" (1 Pet. 1:13-16), and Paul makes it clear that God's will is our sanctification (1 Thess. 4:3).

What I'm opposed to is how progressive sanctification is routinely taught. The undeniable and glorious FACT that we *were* sanctified at salvation and therefore *are* holy right now is usually omitted or side-lined by emphasizing continued sanctification. This is the first thing I disagree with: diminishing the amazing accomplishment of Jesus on the cross.

The second objection I have is that of teaching that we need to *become* holy through our own religious efforts—usually by obeying laws or performing spiritual disciplines.

This gives God's dearly beloved children, whom Jesus has made holy with His sacrifice, the sense that they are not holy before Him. Trying to perfect ourselves in the flesh by obeying laws or performing religious ritual is precisely what Paul calls "another" gospel in the book of Galatians (Gal. 2:21; Gal. 3:1-3). Surely we are participators in the process of our sanctification in that we "walk in the Spirit" and "walk in Him", but we cannot make ourselves good enough nor could we ever do enough good to make *ourselves* holier than the blood of Jesus already did and does. What we should be teaching is the good news that we are right now holy and that this present holiness and continued growth in holiness are BOTH His doing. (Please also see Day 5.)

> ### *Hebrews 10:10 Amplified*
> *And in accordance with this will [of God], we have been made holy (consecrated and sanctified) through the offering made once for all of the body of Jesus Christ (the Anointed One).*
> ### *1 Thessalonians 5:23-24*
> *Now may the God of peace Himself sanctify you completely; and may your whole spirit, soul, and body be preserved blameless at the coming of our Lord Jesus Christ. ²⁴ He who calls you is faithful, who also will do it.*

Q: Are you saying it is wrong to tithe?
A: It is wrong to tithe if you are doing it as a law or in order to get blessed or avoid being cursed. However, if you "purpose in your heart" to give a certain percentage not grudgingly or of necessity, this is acceptable. If you are unable to give a certain percentage or to give anything at all there should be no guilt associated with it. Some people have no money to give. Let them give their time. No time or money? Then be kind. Pray for someone. Give what you are able to give and what you want to give. The amount is not what Jesus sees. He sees your heart. Giving should bring you joy.

Mark 12:41-44

Now Jesus sat opposite the treasury and saw how the people put money into the treasury. And many who were rich put in much. ⁴² Then one poor widow came and threw in two mites, which make a quadrans. ⁴³ So He called His disciples to Himself and said to them, "Assuredly, I say to you that this poor widow has put in more than all those who have given to the treasury; ⁴⁴ for they all put in out of their abundance, but she out of her poverty put in all that she had, her whole livelihood."

Q: Are you against the traditional organized church?

A: Receiving the message of the good news of Jesus is what is most important and we recommend people find a place of fellowship where the true gospel is being proclaimed no matter what the format may be. Some have "left" the organized church for something more "organic" only to find that their new gathering is also teaching mixture. The most important things to find in a fellowship are that the true gospel is being taught without mixture and that everything that happens within that structure be done in love.

Day 29

A GREAT CLOUD OF WITNESSES

*A*s I've penned this work, I have been keenly aware of my audience as one with a variety of understandings on this topic. I know that there are those among you who simply needed to read what you already knew and believed. For you, this book has been another confirmation among many others of what God has already been teaching you.

Others have read these pages as a means of rediscovering that the gospel really is *good* news and it has set you free once again—free to believe that what Jesus did for us is as wonderfully and beautifully true as He proclaimed it to be. I join Paul and pray that you will continue in His grace and become fully established in it!

If you are like we were, though, you might still be skeptical, and we don't blame you. It is right and necessary to "prove all things and hold fast to that which is good." We ask you to dig deeper into what Jesus accomplished *for* us. Don't listen only to those who are currently preaching against "grace extremists" and who refer to their teachings as "hyper-grace", and don't be turned away by some "grace" teachers who have veered off into heresy. Keep reading other authors on this topic such as the ones we recommend at the end of this book. We pray for you to see it, for your eyes to be reopened to how amazingly bountiful is His grace.

Along the way, we have encountered those who strongly oppose what we are teaching. We have been viewed as the very enemies of God who are "watering down the gospel". As Paul persecuted the early church feeling that he was doing the will of God and protecting what He believed, even today there are those among the church who consider the gospel of God's grace as described in these pages to be heresy, plain and simple. These will criticize the message of God's grace. They will go out of their way to defame and even to destroy these truths (and those who proclaim them) thinking they are doing God's service. If this describes you, we pray that God will reveal His true gospel to you on your way to Damascus. We forgive you and love you in Jesus name.

It's also apparent that this book hasn't been written in a private space where only those who minister and teach in the church may gather. Alongside us as I write and you read, I have been keenly aware of God's sheep listening on; those to whom we've been called to minister. Each week they get up and go to church, laying aside their need for a full day off or their desire to take the family on an outing. They come, some out of tradition, some out of guilt, and most with a strong desire that something that is said this week will give them hope. What do most of them hear? "God is good. You are not. Ask for forgiveness. Go and sin no more." Imagine the horrid impact of hearing this week after week, year after year after year! This endless formula of pointing out what is wrong with people and then prescribing a formula for future success based on law, defines precisely what it means to preach "another" gospel. Yes, we were born again by the Spirit, but now *we* have to perfect *ourselves*? This is not only bad news instead of good news; it is heresy.

Shall we not instead share with the sheep what JESUS has done for them, how He has set them free—how much He loves them and of how much He wants to give them? *This* is the glad tidings of good things. We *are* righteous. We *are* holy, blameless, and without reproach. We *are* dearly beloved children of the living God. We *are* joint heirs with Christ. We *are* free from sin because we are under grace not law. We *have* eternal life. God is not mad at us. He loves us.

He is in us and we are in Him; perfectly close. Nothing, even and especially not our sin, can separate us from His love.

The Christian life is NOT about what *we* do.
It's about what HE did.
He started it and HE will complete it.

So, dear sheep, just as I've asked if we the church are preaching "another" gospel, now, I ask you, if you, the church, are hearing and believing and even beginning to teach "another" gospel? I know many pastors and have tremendous respect for them and their labor of love. With all of their hearts they are endeavoring to give you the truth, but no matter how much you love and trust them, no matter how noble and sincere your teachers may be, you have a responsibility to "prove all things and hold fast to that which is good".

It isn't "touching God's anointed" to disagree with what you are taught or to have opinions about how your pastors treat the sheep. You aren't out of "unity" if you speak what is true for our unity is based on the *faith*, not on agreeing. Just because your pastor has gone to Bible college and has multiple degrees does not mean he is more qualified to understand the gospel than you. Perhaps you've heard, as we have, the analogy that no one would try to tell his surgeon how to do surgery, so why do you question your pastor who has more knowledge and training than you? Yet, wouldn't you challenge even your surgeon if he proposed removing one of your vital organs? Consider this: your pastor *isn't* a surgeon and you aren't his patient. You are both children of God, both anointed, and both capable of understanding the gospel of the grace of God.

The time of pastoral intimidation is over. The church is not a theocracy! It's a group of people who have joined together to believe in Jesus and love each other. Yes, God appoints overseers within the body of Christ, but there is one head of the church and His name is Jesus. The rest of us are His beloved body, and we are working *together*, each of us doing what we are called to do. Some of us will be prophets, evangelist, apostles, pastors, and teachers who will *serve* the body to build it up. Others will have other gifts named in Scripture. However, not one of us is ever to lord it over another. In the world we live under hierarchies, but not in the body of Christ.

Paul warned the sheep about the teachers in Galatia who were teaching them "another" gospel and I am warning you. It's important to hold tightly to the truth. May God open your eyes and use you to help those who teach you to understand. May God give you confidence to speak the truth in love.

Ephesians 4:11-16
*And He Himself gave some to be apostles, some prophets, some evangelists, and some pastors and teachers, *[12]* for the equipping of the saints for the work of ministry, for the edifying of the body of Christ, *[13]* till we all come to the unity of the faith and of the knowledge of the Son of God, to a perfect man, to the measure of the stature of the fullness of Christ; *[14]* that we should no longer be children, tossed to and fro and carried about with every wind of doctrine, by the trickery of men, in the cunning craftiness of deceitful plotting, *[15]* but, **speaking the truth in love**, may grow up in all things into Him who is the head—Christ— *[16]* from whom the whole body, joined and knit together by what every joint supplies, according to the effective working by which every part does its share, causes growth of the body for the edifying of itself in love.*

Day 30

TRUTH OR CONSEQUENCES

 S ince we never saw preaching "another" gospel as meaning anything more than the false doctrines taught by cults, we never felt concerned about Paul declaring that anyone who preaches such a gospel is "accursed". What used to worry us more was the following verse.

James 3:1
My brethren, let not many of you become teachers, knowing that we shall receive a stricter judgment.

God went to great extents to give us *His* gospel. We need to get it right. He doesn't want us to add to it or subtract from it.[71] If we are called as teachers, it is crucial that we share *the* gospel, the *whole* gospel, and *nothing* but the gospel with God's beloved sheep, not only because this is His bidding, but because we will give an account for what we teach.

It *does* matter what we teach. What we teach builds on the body of Christ. If we build well, our work will remain and

---

[71] Adding to the gospel would be to add requirements beyond grace and faith, such as law or works. Subtracting from the gospel would be something such as saying that because we are perfectly forgiven, it is ok to sin.

we will be rewarded. If we don't, our work will be lost along with our reward.

1 Corinthians 3:9-17

For we are God's fellow workers; you (plural) are God's field, you (plural) are God's building. [10] According to the grace of God which was given to me, as a wise master builder I have laid the foundation, and another builds on it. **But let each one take heed how he builds on it.** *[11] For no other foundation can anyone lay than that which is laid, which is* **Jesus Christ***. [12] Now if anyone builds on this foundation with gold, silver, precious stones, wood, hay, straw, [13] each one's work will become clear; for the Day will declare it, because it will be revealed by fire; and the fire will test each one's work, of what sort it is.[14] If anyone's work which he has built on it endures, he will receive a reward. [15] If anyone's work is burned, he will suffer loss; but he himself will be saved, yet so as through fire. [16] Do you not know that you (plural) are the temple of God and that the Spirit of God dwells in you (plural)? [17]* **If anyone defiles the temple of God, God will destroy him.** *For the temple of God is holy, which temple you (plural) are.*

This passage is directed primarily at those who labor in the building of the body of Christ (v 7). The temple spoken of in verses 16-17 is the body of Christ. If you are called to build upon the foundation of the body of Christ, God is going to reward you for doing it well and "destroy" you if you don't. You will still be saved (v 15), but your work will be consumed.

When we stand before Christ, we, those who build, will be held to a higher standard. If we feed His sheep the true gospel (gold, silver, and precious stones) our work will remain. If we teach "another" gospel (wood, hay, and straw) our work will be lost.

245

Since Jesus also told Peter to "care" for the sheep, then how we treat God's flock will also be something for which we give an account. The many horror stories we've heard about how abusively some pastors treat those whom God has put in their care, breaks our hearts. Many people have been *devastated* by their spiritual overseers, some of them so deeply that they vow to never enter a church again.

Brethren, these things should never happen, but they do.[72] So many pastors forget these warnings and admonitions. They disregard that Jesus is the head of the church, not they themselves.

Luke 17:1-2
*Then He said to the disciples, "It is impossible that no offenses should come, but **woe to him through whom they do come**!* [2] *It would be better for him if a millstone were hung around his neck, and he were thrown into the sea, than that he should offend one of these little ones.*

Matthew 23:1-12
Then Jesus spoke to the multitudes and to His disciples, [2] *saying: "The scribes and the Pharisees sit in Moses' seat.* [3] *Therefore whatever they tell you to observe, that observe and do, but do not do according to their works; for they say, and do not do.* [4] *For they bind heavy burdens, hard to bear, and lay them on men's shoulders; but they themselves will not move them with one of their fingers.* [5] *But all their works they do to be seen by men. They make their phylacteries broad and enlarge the borders of their garments.* [6] *They love the best places at feasts, the best seats in the synagogues,* [7] *greetings in the marketplaces, and to be called by men, 'Rabbi,*

---

[72] If you have been a victim of spiritual abuse or you are a pastor who wants to avoid these types of things happening in your church or need to counsel someone who has been hurt in the past by someone in ministry, we highly recommend <u>The Subtle Power of Spiritual Abuse</u> by Jeff VanVonderen.

Rabbi.' [8] *But you, do not be called 'Rabbi'; for One is your Teacher, the Christ, and you are all brethren.* [9] *Do not call anyone on earth your father; for One is your Father, He who is in heaven.* [10] *And do not be called teachers; for One is your Teacher, the Christ.* [11] *But he who is greatest among you shall be your servant.* [12] *And whoever exalts himself will be humbled, and he who humbles himself will be exalted.*

Philippians 2:5-7

Let this mind be in you which was also in Christ Jesus, [6] *who, being in the form of God, did not consider it robbery to be equal with God,* [7] *but made Himself of no reputation, taking the form of a bondservant, and coming in the likeness of men.*

1 Peter 5:1-4

The elders who are among you I exhort, I who am a fellow elder and a witness of the sufferings of Christ, and also a partaker of the glory that will be revealed: [2] *Shepherd the flock of God which is among you, serving as overseers,* **not by compulsion but willingly, not for dishonest gain but eagerly;** [3] **nor as being lords over those entrusted to you, but being examples to the flock;** [4] *and when the Chief Shepherd appears, you will receive the crown of glory that does not fade away.*

Dear friends, we are called to build upon the foundation of Jesus Christ. What an awesome trust He has given us. God's people are His temple. If we defile them by false teaching or mistreatment, we will give an account before God. It would be unjust of God to overlook these things.

You might say, "Well, that doesn't sound like 'grace' to me," but it profoundly is. The fact that someone who has taught "another" gospel or who has mistreated God's sheep will have his works burned but still be saved is amazing grace indeed for God deeply loves and identifies with His children, but who among us wants to stand before Jesus with a pile of ashes at our feet? If you have been trusted with the care of God's people, be sure that you love them with His love and teach them the true gospel.

Day 31

THE GOSPEL, THE WHOLE GOSPEL, AND NOTHING BUT THE GOSPEL

Romans 10:15
How beautiful are the feet of those who preach the gospel of peace,
Who bring glad tidings of good things!"

*T*hroughout this book, I've been asking you to consider if we, the church, are preaching "another" gospel by mixing law with grace and teaching formula living instead of a Spirit-led life. I've done my best to point out in what ways I believe we are teaching "another". Now, as I draw to a close, another question is rising in my heart, "Are we preaching *the* gospel, the whole gospel, and nothing but the gospel?" After all, we are ministers of *the* "gospel". Are we preaching the gospel of grace and peace, the *glad* tidings of *good* things, or are we presenting our new birth as only a *catalyst* for change instead of the change itself?

As Paul neared the end of his letter to the Galatians, he wrote the following moving verses.

Galatians 6:11-15
*As many as desire to make a good showing in the flesh, these would compel you to be circumcised, only **that they may not suffer persecution for***

the cross of Christ. *[13] For not even those who are circumcised* **keep the law,**[73] *but they desire to have you circumcised that they may boast in your flesh.* **[14] But God forbid that I should boast except in the cross of our Lord Jesus Christ, by whom the world has been crucified to me, and I to the world.** *[15] For in Christ Jesus neither circumcision nor uncircumcision avails anything, but a new creation.*

What is the gospel? It is the good news of what God the Father accomplished through the death, burial, and resurrection of God the Son, Jesus Christ. It is about Jesus and His death and resurrection. It is about a new creation. That is what we preach. When we know who we are and what we have in Him as a result of His cross; in other words, when we realize that we are new creations, we will grow and become strong in Him by grace through faith.

Philemon 1:4-6

I thank my God, making mention of you always in my prayers, [5] hearing of your love and faith which you have toward the Lord Jesus and toward all the saints, [6] **that the sharing (fellowship) of your faith may become effective by the acknowledgment of every good thing (benefit) which is in you in Christ Jesus.**

---

[73] Galatians is not only about circumcision and other ceremonial laws as some have supposed. It is about the entire law. We see this evidenced in this verse, but even more so in Galatians 5:3 which reads, "And I testify again to every man who becomes circumcised that he is a debtor to keep the whole law." **The Judaizers wanted to circumcise the Gentiles not only to make a show of their flesh but to obligate them to keep the entire law.** This was apparently also the intent of the sect of the Pharisees in Acts 15 who asserted that, "It is necessary to circumcise them AND to command them to keep the law of Moses".

All that we need in order to truly live and be godly comes through acknowledgment of His grace toward us. In Him we have exceedingly great and precious promises through which we partake of the divine nature.

2 Peter 1:2-4
*Grace and peace be multiplied to you in the knowledge of God and of Jesus our Lord, ³ **as His divine power has given to us all things that pertain to life and godliness, through the knowledge of Him** who called us by glory and virtue, ⁴ by which have been given to us **exceedingly great and precious promises, that through these you may be partakers of the divine nature**, having escaped the corruption that is in the world through lust.*

This is why Paul prayed for believers to have continual revelation of Jesus.

Ephesians 1:17
*Therefore I also, after I heard of your faith in the Lord Jesus and your love for all the saints, ¹⁶ do not cease to give thanks for you, making mention of you in my prayers: ¹⁷ that the God of our Lord Jesus Christ, the Father of glory, **may give (may be giving) to you the spirit of wisdom and revelation in the knowledge of Him**, ¹⁸ the eyes of your understanding (realization) being enlightened (made to see, illuminated); that you may know (perceive): **what is the hope of His calling, what are the riches of the glory of His inheritance in the saints, ¹⁹ and what is the exceeding greatness of His power toward us who believe, according to the working of His mighty power ²⁰ which He worked in Christ when He raised Him from the dead and seated Him at His right hand in the heavenly places, ²¹** far above all principality and power and might and dominion,*

*and every name that is named, not only in this age
but also in that which is to come.*

It's all about Jesus! Even though the ministry of "death"
and "condemnation", the law, was "glorious", we now turn
away from the teachings of Moses as our instruction for
daily living and behold the glory of Jesus and thus we are
transformed into His image by the Spirit of the Lord.

> **2 Corinthians 3:16-18**
> *Nevertheless when one turns to the Lord (in con-
> text—from the law of Moses), the veil is taken away.*
> *¹⁷ Now the Lord is the Spirit; and where the Spirit
> of the Lord is, there is liberty. ¹⁸ But we all, with
> unveiled face, **beholding as in a mirror the glory
> of the Lord, are being transformed into the same
> image from glory to glory, just as by the Spirit
> of the Lord.***

Yes, law can motivate people to change their behaviors,
but with law must also come fear because law motivates
from without. Without the threat of punishment or the
promise of blessing, the law is powerless to produce "right"
living. Jesus (God's grace to us) motivates from within. He
made us new creations where He can now work in us both
to will and to do of His good pleasure. The results of law and
grace may *look* similar, but the law can only bring outward
conformity and death while Jesus is the only One who can
change the heart and give life. When we preach Jesus and
Him crucified we are imparting the power of the gospel to
God's beloved sheep.

There is no need for us to attach prerequisites beyond
faith to receiving God's grace. Yet David and I did this for so
many years, that when we finally recognized that all He provides was ours as a gift, we didn't know what or how to teach.
Our former sermon outlines amounted to these two formulas:
"This is what is wrong with you and this is what you need
to do about it," or "If you want to see A, B, and C in your life

you must fast and pray and read the Bible and live a holy life and give and attend church each time the church doors open and be a good spouse and be a good parent and witness to the lost and become a missionary or become a minister or at least have a small group in your home and turn the other cheek and die daily to self; and when these aren't enough, double your efforts, and if that doesn't work learn how to do these things *better!*" We profoundly recognize now that these messages fell flat in light of Jesus Christ and His cross. If you happened to fall victim to this kind of thinking while a part of our ministry, we sincerely apologize, and we pray that God will open your eyes to His glorious gospel of grace.

As Pentecostals, David and I focused so much on the *dunamis* of the Holy Spirit that we seldom reflected on the *dunamis of the gospel.*

Romans 1:16-17
For I am not ashamed of the gospel of Christ, for it is the power (dunamis—miraculous power) of God to salvation for everyone who believes, for the Jew first and also for the Greek. ¹⁷ For in it the righteousness of God is revealed from faith to faith; as it is written, "The just shall live by faith."

We can trust that when we preach the gospel, the whole gospel, and nothing but the gospel, that it is the miraculous power of God. It goes into the heart and brings about revelation and change without the need for law.

Hebrews 4:12
For the word of God (the gospel) is living and powerful, and sharper than any two-edged sword, piercing even to the division of soul and spirit, and of joints and marrow, and is a discerner of the thoughts and intents of the heart.

This can set us free from thinking we need to single-handedly "fix" everyone and "solve" all of their problems.

Perhaps you have realized, as did we, how difficult and tiring it is attempting to be the Father, Son, and Holy Spirit in the lives of others. When we teach the pure gospel without mixture, we can rest assured that the Holy Spirit is leading the people to whom we minister. He is as surely in them as He is in us. We can trust Him to work out His will in their lives without the need for us to take over. Remember also, that it is the grace of God, not law, that teaches us. When we share the grace of God purely it will instruct the hearer to deny worldly lusts and to live sensibly. Attempting to "balance" the grace of God by adding conditions other than faith in Jesus and Him crucified is to nullify the cross.

We need to focus on teaching *the* gospel; the glad tidings of good things from our great and good God that bring great joy! We must teach that God's gifts are truly unmerited and truly free. Salvation, forgiveness, righteousness, holiness, provision, health, and everything He gives is free to those who believe in the Son—no if, ands, or buts!

Sitting in churches right now are people who have already awakened to grace and recognize, lamentably, that their beloved teachers are preaching "another" gospel. I am convinced that they are praying for them to "get it", to understand that the gospel is good enough and needs no additives so that they may continue with their local assembly in the work of the ministry.

Sadly, we have seen many people feel the need to leave their beloved church community because the ministry there was a mixture of law and grace. We've seen how difficult it is for them and how some of them have even been shunned by family and friends for their decision as if the church were a cult. They love their ministers and they love those who attend the fellowship, but simply cannot go on receiving "another" gospel.

Perhaps you have personally experienced people leaving your ministry and have blamed the grace message for what you perceive to be a lack of unity, even love, on the part of those who have embraced it. Yet we all know that the truth both unites *and* divides. It is important to recognize that our unity is not based on people believing what *we* teach, it's based on *the* faith (Eph. 4:13).

If we teach the unadulterated gospel of grace and peace, there will be those who will run interference against us. They will warn of the dangers of getting involved with a "fad", of becoming "unbalanced", of watering down the gospel,[74] of becoming a "grace extremist"[75] or teaching "hyper-grace".[76] What will we do? Will we cave into the pressure to mix the Old Covenant into the New or will we put only new wine into new wineskins?

When my husband and I began "Studies in Grace and Faith" in response to the call to "preach the gospel to the saved" we were concerned that we might run out of teaching material. "Seriously," we mused, "how many sermons can one get out of 'the gospel'?" Wouldn't it be boring, maybe even spiritually unhealthy to only hear one message? However, when we saw that the gospel is the sum of Christ's and the apostles' teachings—the full counsel of God, it opened up infinite possibilities. After four years we are still teaching the gospel of God's grace without mixture[77] and are nowhere near exhausting what can be shared.

We began our teachings in the book of Galatians showing the importance of believing in the New Covenant and not adding law. From there we did a study about the gift of righteousness using Romans 1-8. Oh, the joys of seeing this book for what seemed to be the first time! So many truths opened to us that were such a joy to share. Then we

---

[74] It must be said that "watering down the gospel" is not what we think. We think it means not being hard on the people. However, muting grace while teaching law is a much more accurate definition of watering down the gospel.

[75] If there is anything in heaven and earth that is "extreme", it is the grace of God.

[76] Our English word for "hyper" comes from the Greek word "huper". This prefix is used repeatedly in reference to God's grace. **God's grace IS "hyper". It's more than enough. It exceeds our needs.** See in the Greek Eph. 2:7, 2 Cor. 9:14, Rom. 5:20.

[77] Our teaching materials are available for free online at http://www.graceandfaithministries.org.

taught Ephesians and Colossians which speak of the glories of who Jesus is and what God accomplished in Christ. After that we sought to give a better understanding of Hebrews. In every teaching, we keep our perspective on the cross—the glad tidings of good things, of feeding the sheep instead of beating them into submission, of proclaiming what Jesus did *for* them, how He came to serve them, how deeply He loves them, and of setting them free. We continue to explain sound hermeneutic principles to help those attending understand the context and intent of what is written, and encourage them to "prove all things and hold fast to that which is good". We remove the fear of disagreeing with those who teach while helping people to develop the ability to discern the difference between grace and law so that when they are reading a book, listening to a teacher or studying the Bible, they won't fall prey to a mixed "gospel".

As ministers of the glad tidings of good things we teach the sheep to forsake the Old Covenant way of thinking and to live only in the New Covenant of God's grace. We constantly reinforce that we do not live holy lives in order to *become* holy; we live holy lives because we *are* holy. We live righteously *because* we are righteous. We don't sin as believers *because* we are not sinners. We love *because* we are loved. We give *because* we've received. We forgive *because* we've been forgiven. We pray *because* we *are* close to God.

To put it very succinctly, preaching the gospel of grace is teaching the truth about Jesus and what He accomplished for us *without* adding religious formula (law) in order to obtain, maintain, or improve upon what God has already provided in Christ.

Everything we do in this "new and living way" is a fruit of what Jesus has already accomplished in us. If we see that we lack any fruit of the Spirit, we don't *try* to develop that fruit; we simply focus on Jesus. If we see areas in our lives where we are falling short, we thank God we are forgiven because of Jesus' atoning sacrifice and believe that He is working in us to both desire to do His will and to actually do it. The point is that under the Old Covenant the focus was on the individual and what one needed to do. Under the New, our attention is on Jesus and what He did. As we "turn our eyes upon Jesus", the things of earth "grow strangely dim in the light of His glory and grace."

We are learning there is no need to end every sermon with "—if you will only—". We simply share the good news. When a shepherd feeds his sheep, he doesn't ask them to perform afterwards. He calls them and feeds them. They eat and grow. When we feed the sheep the glad tidings of good things from their loving Father they grow and reproduce. Their lives are filled with joy and life which overflow into the community.

Can you imagine such a place of worship, where people are eager to gather because they know they will be fed good food which will encourage and enable them to live a life of faith in Christ? Imagine a place where people are eager to bring their family and friends because they know they will receive something from Jesus and not more religious shame and an ever-lengthening list of expectations.

I am convinced that most believers already *know* what is wrong with them, where they are falling short, and their own weaknesses. They don't need to be told what *they* need to do about it. If they could fix it, they would have already done so. They need to hear what Jesus did about it.

When I taught the high school Sunday School class as a young adult, I decided that I needed to tell the kids to "get sanctified"! So, being a responsible teacher, I looked up all the Bible verses containing the word "sanctify" as my research. Imagine my shock to find that they were already were sanctified![78] So, I did the responsible thing. When I stood before the class, I explained the above and gave them the good news that they were already sanctified. All of them stared at me or tilted their heads in wonder. I didn't even know how to end the teaching. We all sat amazed.

---

[78] Acts 20:32, Acts 26:18, 1 Cor. 1:2, 6:11, Heb. 10:10, 14

This was one of many moments of light that my husband and I experienced while we walked in confusion. The light would go on and we would think, "Ah ha!" but then we'd go back to our mixed beliefs. Yet, I have to wonder, what would happen in our youth groups today if the youth pastor, instead of telling the kids each week to "get right with God" or instructing them on "how to be a good Christian" actually taught them continually that they *are* right with God by faith in Jesus? Would all hell break loose and the kids run off helter-skelter on sinning sprees, or would not their hearts, like ours, respond to His grace? Instead of placing on them law after law about how to behave, would it be possible that the grace of God which sets us free to not sin would be more powerful to teach them than the law which we now know actually strengthens sin?

Is it possible that we could remove the law-based curricula used in most children's ministries and replace them with grace and truth (Jn. 1:17)? Can we trust God's grace even in our children's lives? Didn't Jesus say to allow them to come to Him and not get in their way? Can you imagine how a lifetime of being taught that God loves them and forgives them would positively affect our children instead of 18 years of hearing that if they do right they will be blessed and if they do wrong, they will not be blessed, even cursed? Instead of beating them constantly with law, what would happen if we repeatedly reminded them of his undeserved favor?

What if parents demonstrated the love and grace of God each and every day to their children—loving them when they don't deserve it and giving to them apart from their performance?

What would happen if husbands and wives began to love each other unconditionally—accepting each other "as is" instead of constantly trying to "fix" each other, giving without demanding, communicating without manipulating, encouraging each other instead of constantly criticizing? Can you see what a difference grace, unmerited favor, can make in a relationship?

What about the worship team? Do they understand the grace of God or are they still bringing up songs about the Old Covenant way of worship? Are they begging God to do what He's already done? Are they singing dirge-like melodies that sound more like a funeral procession than a celebration of life? Are the songs about us and what we are determined to do or about Jesus and what He accomplished? Are they relying on manipulative methods to "usher in the presence of God" not recognizing that His presence is in each individual and is there when we gather in His name? What will happen when we sing songs about His love for us and our love for each other; songs of faith instead of fear? Can you picture the exaltation in of a room full of people who are fully aware of God's love for them and living in the joy and rest He promised?

Another matter that I think is relevant is that we needn't be afraid to put a stop to non-Biblical behavior during our meetings. We'll be accused of "quenching the Spirit", but we are mature enough and discerning enough to know the difference between the Holy Spirit and "strange fire". When people understand that mystic nonsense will not be allowed among us, they will either go where they can express their weirdness or awaken to grace and find true satisfaction.

What about the church bookstore? Let someone who fully knows the gospel review books and remove them if necessary. This is not to say that we are trying to ban books because people can buy books from many sources and are free to read whatever they want. We, though, need to be careful what we make available to those who attend our fellowships.

The grace of God will change everything in a church. One may find that many of the programs and ministries in one's church were born out of Old Covenant thinking. From the mission statement to the Constitution and Bylaws to where we spend our time and money and even how we relate to and counsel the people of our gatherings—we need to allow the gospel of the grace of God to renovate it all.

Some of us need to get out of God's way and serve instead of rule[79] and allow ourselves to express God's love to the members of our congregations in personal ways. We need to set aside anything we've been taught about "professional distance".[80] That is not of God. We must be real, open, sincere, available, a friend; especially to those who work with us in ministry. I'm not saying we are required to share our personal affairs with everyone in the church, but that we need to be *genuine* people. If we've been put on a pedestal, it's time to step down. If we in any way think we are superior due to our education, credentials, degrees, or position in the local assembly, we need to consider the example of Jesus who with even higher qualifications (that of being God), humbled Himself to serve us (Phil. 2:5-8).

All we need to do is speak the truth of the gospel in love for it is the miraculous power (dunamis) of God for those who believe—for Christians. God's beloved people already have the Holy Spirit inside of them, and they will hear God speaking His love through us. It might take some time for those who have only seen Christianity as a system of formulas and disciplines to actually understand what the Spirit is saying to them, but with our patience and His grace, they will hear.

Would it be so painful to give it a try—to prove all things? Teach a sermon series that magnifies Jesus and imparts grace to the hearers without "balancing", without tagging on conditions, and just see how those who listen respond. Instead of trying to squeeze something out of people, *give* something to them. Do this week after week, and you will begin to see authentic revival in the lives of those you serve.

Don't be surprised if you meet with opposition. Persecution always follows the preaching of the cross. Rejoice and be exceedingly glad. Great is your reward in heaven. Keep preaching His grace. Don't turn back to a mixture of law and grace because that's what you are used

---

[79] If the shoe fits, wear it; if not, ignore.

[80] Jesus did NOT practice "professional distance".

to believing or because you are afraid of rejection by family and friends. The old is *not* "good enough" nor is it "better". Press forward into His glorious gospel without fear and with faith knowing that it is by knowing the truth that God's people are set free!

Epilogue

W hen steeped in an extensive list of spiritual disciplines, formula, and good works as the very definition and proof of our spirituality and involved in teaching
others to do the same, a book such as this would have either
set us free to return to our first love or been met with much
disagreement. So, we understand either response. Still, we
trust the power of the gospel to reach your heart as it finally
reached ours, and I thank-you for allowing me to share with
you what God has opened our eyes to see.

What you've read in a few days took us many years
to be able to process and later be able to express as we
waded through countless teachings we'd heard or taught
based on a mixture of law and grace. Some of these "truths"
were so sacred to me (having grown up "in the church") that
I strongly resisted giving them any serious consideration
for many years, even after already understanding that we'd
taken a wrong turn in our walk with Jesus. Believe me when
I say that I understand how difficult it is to even contemplate
that some of our most sacred beliefs and practices are
nothing more than man-made traditions or leftovers from an
obsolete covenant. I lovingly encourage you to place this all
before the Lord and ask Him to reveal the truth of the gospel
of God's grace to you.

May the Lord set us all completely free from "another"
gospel and give us boldness to proclaim the true gospel—the

gospel of God's grace, peace, and love, one that is not only for the lost, but for us, His beloved children.

Thank-you for listening and for hearing.

Grace and peace to you with love!

Romans 16:25-27
Now to Him who is able to establish you according to my gospel and the preaching of Jesus Christ, according to the revelation of the mystery kept secret since the world began [26] but now made manifest, and by the prophetic Scriptures made known to all nations, according to the commandment of the everlasting God, for obedience to the faith— [27] to God, alone wise, be glory through Jesus Christ forever. Amen.

What We Refuse to Believe or Teach

- ✒ *We refuse to believe that something beyond faith in God's grace can save us.*

- ✒ *We refuse to form our beliefs and teaching based on Consensus Christianity (what is accepted as true but isn't) instead of upon the written word of God.*

- ✒ *We refuse to believe that spiritual disciplines maintain or improve our righteousness or holiness.*

- ✒ *We refuse to see ourselves as "only sinners saved by grace".*

- ✒ *We refuse to believe that forgiveness is something we need to obtain.*

- ✒ *We refuse to believe we have a sinful nature.*

- ✒ *We refuse to mix the Old Covenant with the New.*

- ✒ *We refuse to live under the blessings and curses of the law.*

- ✒ *We refuse to cultivate in ourselves a spirit of hunger, thirst, or desperation.*

❧ *We refuse to believe that we need to obtain, maintain, or improve our closeness with God.*

❧ *We refuse to see ourselves as outside of God's presence or His presence as outside of us.*

❧ *We refuse to turn Christ's command to love each other into a mere addition to an already long list of "Christian" duties.*

❧ *We refuse to nullify the gospel of the grace of God by adding conditions to receiving it.*

❧ *We refuse to beat God's beloved sheep.*

❧ *We refuse to redefine terms to make our relationship with God the opposite of what He intends for it to be.*

❧ *We refuse to focus on how we must prove our love for God by trying to pay Him back for what He has freely given us.*

❧ *We refuse to believe that we need to continually put ourselves to death.*

❧ *We refuse to ever see ourselves separated from God or His love for us.*

❧ *We refuse to believe that God's love for us is based on what we do or do not do.*

❧ *We are determined to teach the gospel, the whole gospel, and nothing but the gospel.*

Further Discussion

If you'd like to discuss topics covered in this book, feel free to "Like" my Page at:

https://www.facebook.com/cdhildebrandgrace

Studies in Grace and Faith

SGF is a teaching ministry focused on helping believers return to their first love through better understanding the gospel of the grace of God. Believers gather together for a meal and fellowship, listen to a DVD teaching which normally includes communion and a song or two. After viewing the DVD the activities in the group vary from sharing testimonies, praying for each other, extended worship, or simply more fellowship. Detailed notes are also provided.

These teachings are an excellent resource for individual or a small group study. If you or your place of fellowship would like to be part of SGF or use our materials, simply go to our website[81] where all you need to get started is provided free of charge. There is no requirement to "join" us, but we will be delighted to know that you have. Simply leave a comment letting us know you've begun and where you are located as an encouragement to this ministry.

---

[81] http://www.graceandfaithministries.org

Grace and Faith Awakening

Grace and Faith Awakening[82] is an outreach to local churches with the gospel of the grace of God. We believe that authentic revival comes when we:

- Rediscover our first love—God's love for us,
- Understand what He accomplished and who we are in Him, and
- Identify false religious traditions which turn the one true gospel into "another".

A Grace and Faith Awakening takes place in the following sequence:

- Outreach to existing senior pastors (a necessary first step)
- Assisting the pastor in educating the church ministry team (in order to encourage unity of the faith)
- Grace and Faith Awakening 1-3 day conference (length of time depends on your needs and our availability)
- On-going education via Studies in Grace and Faith

If you are a senior pastor who is interested in the Grace and Faith Awakening sequence, please send a private message to me on my Facebook page, C. D. Hildebrand, at https://www.facebook.com/cdhildebrandgrace. Please leave your name, the name of your church, website address (if available), and how we may best contact you. We look forward to partnering with you as your church awakens to God's glorious gospel of grace.

---

[82] Grace and Faith Awakening is part of Studies in Grace and Faith which is an approved teaching ministry with the Northern California Nevada District of the Assemblies of God.

Recommended Reading

Classic Christianity: Life's too Short to Miss the Real Thing
by Bob George

Classic Christianity Illustrated by Bob George

Destined to Reign: The Secret to Effortless Success,
Wholeness and Victorious Living by Joseph Prince

Destined to Reign Devotional: Daily Reflections for
Effortless Success, Wholeness and Victorious Living by
Joseph Prince

Families Where Grace is in Place: Building a Home Free of
Manipulation, Legalism, and Shame by Jeff VanVonderen

52 Lies Heard in Church Every Sunday: And Why the Truth
Is So Much Better by Steve McVey

Fight for Grace: It's Time to Roll Up Your Sleeves by
Andrew Nelson

Be Free (Galatians): Exchange Legalism for True Spirituality
by Warren Weirsbe

The Gospel in Ten Words by Paul Ellis

The Gospel Uncut: Learning to Rest in the Grace of God by
Jeremy White

The Grace Awakening: Believing in grace is one thing. Living
it is another. by Charles Swindoll

Grace Awakening Workbook by Charles Swindoll

He Loves Me!—Learning to Live in the Father's Affection by
Wayne Jacobsen

Jesus Changes Everything: It's Time to Embrace God's
Unconditional Love by Bob George

Love Revolution—Rediscovering the Lost Command of
Jesus by Gaylord Enns

The Naked Gospel: The Truth You May Never Hear in
Church by Andrew Farley

The Prodigal God by Timothy Keller

The Subtle Power of Spiritual Abuse: Recognizing and
Escaping Spiritual Manipulation and False Spiritual
Authority within the Church by Jeff VanVonderen

The War is Over: God is Not Mad, So Stop Struggling with
Sin and Judgment by Andrew Wommack

CPSIA information can be obtained at www.ICGtesting.com
Printed in the USA
BVOW03s2031220114

342718BV00006B/15/P